W9-CPB-806

HINSDALE
PUBLIC LIBRARY

Capture the Flag

Capture the Flag

The Stars and Stripes in American History

Arnaldo Testi

Translated by Noor Giovanni Mazhar

NEW YORK UNIVERSITY PRESS *New York and London*

NEW YORK UNIVERSITY PRESS

NEW YORK AND LONDON
WWW.NYUPRESS.ORG

Library of Congress Cataloging-in-Publication Data
Testi, Arnaldo. [Stelle e strisce. English] Capture the flag : the stars and stripes in American history /

Arnaldo Testi ; translated by Noor Giovanni Mazhar.
p. cm. Originally published in Italian by Bollati Boringhieri Editore in 2003.

Includes bibliographical references and index.
ISBN-13: 978-0-8147-8322-1 (cloth : alk. paper)
ISBN-10: 0-8147-8322-8 (cloth : alk. paper)

1. Flags—United States—History. 2. Flags—Social aspects—United States. 3. National characteristics, American. 4. Patriotism—United States—History. 5. Political culture—United States—History. 6. United States—History—Miscellanea. 7. United States—History, Military—Miscellanea. I. Title.

CR113.T4613 2010 929.9'20973—DC22 2009039278

New York University Press books are printed on acid-free paper, and their binding materials are chosen for strength and durability. We strive to use environmentally responsible suppliers and materials to the greatest extent possible in publishing our books.

Manufactured in the United States of America
10 9 8 7 6 5 4 3 2 1

This flag which we honor and under which we serve is the emblem of our unity, our power, our thought and purpose as a nation. It has no other character than that which we give it from generation to generation. The choices are ours. It floats in majestic silence above the hosts that execute those choices, whether in peace or war. And yet, though silent, it speaks to us.

—Woodrow Wilson, "Flag Day Address" (June 14, 1917)

We have two American flags always: one for the rich and one for the poor. When the rich fly it it means that things are under control; when the poor fly it it means danger, revolution, anarchy.

—Henry Miller, *The Air-Conditioned Nightmare* (1945)

It might be said that we all draw something from our national symbol, for it is capable of conveying simultaneously a spectrum of meanings.

—U.S. Supreme Court, *Spence v. Washington*, 418 U.S. 405 (1974)

Contents

Acknowledgments

Three people were special in this enterprise. Claudio Pavone, of the University of Pisa, asked me to write my first essay on the U.S. flag for his journal, *Parolechiave*. Alfredo Salsano, who is now no longer with us, saw the potential for a book in my essay and insisted that I should do it for his publishing house, Bollati Boringhieri in Turin. Ellen Carol DuBois, of the University of California–Los Angeles, encouraged me to translate and publish the book in English and found the way to make it happen. Then there are Susan Crile and David Thelen, who have been generous hosts and interlocutors during my research journeys in the United States, respectively, in New York City and Bloomington, Indiana. There is the unknown Manhattan lady who explained to me (rather confusedly, as is understandable) why she was wearing a flag pin after September 11 and then donated it to me. There are the anonymous reviewers and the editorial staff at NYU Press, who helped in improving the original text and produced a beautiful artifact. Finally, there are the students in my class of American history in Pisa, who were the first, in the winter of 2001–2, to formulate the question that was the starting point of my research: What do Americans do when they display the Stars and Stripes? Or to paraphrase the beautiful title of a Raymond Carver short story, what do they talk about when they talk about the flag? The answer to this simple question has been neither simple nor quick, and it could not be otherwise. Just as I was jotting down the first notes of my work, in the spring of 2003, my fellow citizens covered their balconies with rainbow flags in protest against the war in Iraq, showing me how the popular passion for a flag can spread but also confusing me with the various reasons that they gave for doing so (what exactly did Italians do when they displayed the peace rainbow flag?). I also learned the complexities of flag passions from two very dear persons, my father, *il professore* Enrico, and my wife

Marina's grandfather, *il maestro* Menotti Bennati, who in different ways and at different times in their lives placed their trust in the red flag (what exactly were Italians doing when they were displaying the red flag?). To their memory, I dedicated the Italian edition of this book, as I now also dedicate this revised and enlarged American edition.

Introduction *Totem*

The Stars and Stripes is the totem of the nation, the sacred emblem of a shared national faith or civic religion. The flag is omnipresent in public and private places, in institutional as well as communal and domestic settings, in entertainment and commercial venues and products. The flag is surrounded by taboos: it has to be treated in accordance with precise rules of protocol, and whoever does not respect them can provoke horror and scandal. And yet it is so powerful as to protect, in the name of the principles that it represents, even those who deface or burn it. The flag stirs up strong personal and political emotions: cohesion, belonging, pride, individual and collective identity, anger and revenge against enemies or traitors, anger against the government itself. And it expects strong responses: the loyalty of the citizens' bodies, the devotion of their minds, the love of their hearts. The flag is the revered object of periodical rituals, of actual prayers such as the morning school salute and the recitation of the Pledge of Allegiance. In extraordinary circumstances, the ubiquity of the flag and the emotions it inspires explode to extraordinary dimensions. It happened after the September 11, 2001, attacks, the event that first sparked my interest in writing this book. And yet its very extraordinariness only serves to exalt ordinary practices—ordinary practices that are so much a part of the landscape that they may go unnoticed by the natives but that to many foreigners seem conspicuous and excessive, lacking in irony and self-irony; to me they seem embarrassing for their lack of reserve. Native and foreign observers often agree about the very special status of the national flag in the consciousness of the American people, about a unique, exceptional American "flag fetishism," unlike that of any other people. Of all countries, according to British social psychologist Michael Billig, "the United States is arguably today the home of what Renan called 'the cult of the flag.'"[1]

The Stars and Stripes, though, is not unique in its status as a totem, in arousing intense cults and fetishisms. Other flags have similar claims, around the world. In the heat of the 2006 so-called Mohammed cartoons controversy, another dramatic event that sustained my curiosity in flag history and culture, Danish flags joined American flags at widespread flag-burning demonstrations across the Muslim world. And Danes reacted with shock and sorrow: because, they said, the national colors, affectionately called *Dannebrog,* or "Danish cloth," are dear to their hearts, a banner of joy, solidarity, community, and family celebration—a people's banner as well as the state's.[2] Actually, all the flags of the Scandinavian countries, like that of Great Britain, for that matter, are beloved, domesticated, commercialized, and sacralized objects. They are routinely hoisted on public buildings, homes, churches, and department stores and posted on goods, both sacred and profane—such as the classical Union Jack underwear. Many believe that there are no countries in the world with so many flagpoles as in Scandinavia.[3] The sacralization of these flags seems more readily understandable than that of the Stars and Stripes. After all, their designs (a variety of crosses) and their mythical origins (they are narrated as ancient gifts from the pope or heaven or God herself) are firmly rooted in the Christian faith. Many national flags, indeed, display outright religious symbols: the Japanese Shinto Sun Goddess and the Indian Chakra or Buddhist spinning wheel, the Muslim countries' color green and Israel's tallith, or prayer shawl. In these cases, defacement is literally "desecration," often forbidden and sometimes punished.[4] The Stars and Stripes, the French *Tricouleur* and the Red flag, and their offspring all over the world are among the few flags born secular because engendered by revolutions, either already accomplished or promised. They did not remain secular for long, though. When they became established state flags, they were quickly absorbed into national, civil religions and political theologies and supplied with adequate myths of origins. It is surprising how little is known of how, when, and by whom they were actually invented. Mysterious births add to their mystique.[5]

Since the Stars and Stripes' mysterious birth in the late 1770s, in Betsy Ross's womb, its totemic cult (as I show in part 1 of this book) grew slowly over a century and half; and some of its rites of worship are quite recent indeed. The cult has been developed and is administered from above, by a set of ministers and priests chosen for this purpose. They are, as can easily be imagined, the leading figures of the political and military state institutions, and what they display and honor is the official flag. Nevertheless, the representatives of the institutions are not the only ones to do so, and often, historically, they were not the first to have done so. The flag is also the icon of popular nationalisms that are nourished by heartfelt adherence, deep convictions, sentimental fervor, and melodramatic sentimentality. Many demonstrations linked to the flag were, in effect, born autonomously, outside the sphere of state officialdom, and only later absorbed, regulated, and codified by the latter. That public institutions did not play an active role in initiating patriotic rituals appears to many observers a peculiarly American phenomenon, the confirmation of an old transatlantic conviction: the supremacy, in the United States, of civil society over a state that, compared to other modern states, is weak and distant.[6] I am not so sure. It seems to me that, on the one hand, in Europe as in the transatlantic world and perhaps in the Far East, rituals and cults of this type emerged, in the crucial years between the nineteenth century and the beginning of the twentieth, due, undoubtedly, to a complex web of state initiatives but also to groups, associations, and movements from below,[7] and that, on the other hand, state agencies did not refrain from doing their part in the United States. The important thing is to look in the right direction, at the right moment. In the United States, around 1900, power resided above all in the capitals of the individual states of the Union, not in the federal capital. And many of those states fairly quickly adopted the flag festivities. After 1900, things changed, and the federal government also intervened. And it did so with ever-greater incisiveness as it gradually acquired a new authority, which it had not had in the previous century and which began to be perceived and exercised, both in practical terms and symbolically, as truly national.

The Stars and Stripes is a multifaceted totem. It is a flag both of freedom and of empire (as I suggest in parts 2 and 3). But what *freedom* and *empire* mean, and what constitutes their reciprocal relationship, is the object and the very essence of American history and of the controversies that have molded it. This, too, is not an exceptional situation. The United States was born from a revolution that, like other modern revolutions (from the French Revolution to the Bolshevik one, including the third transatlantic revolution, the second revolution in the Americas, the first Black revolution—that of Haiti), saw itself as a traumatic generative event, as a new beginning not only in national history but also in world history. All revolutions have aspired to this universality, and they have not been too fastidious about the means they adopted to achieve it, to re-create the world in their own image and likeness. They did it with the soft power of ideas, ideals, and influence, with the hard power of armies and power politics, often with imperial and colonial policies, authoritarian, Napoleonic, Stalinist.[8] The Spirit of '76 was the announcement of a project of freedom, of freedom and sovereignty for the new United States, of individual freedoms for the former colonists, but also of freedom for the whole of humankind. Of course, nobody put it better than Tom Paine: "We have it in our power to begin the world over again. A situation, similar to the present, hath not happened since the days of Noah until now." And again: "The cause of America is in a great measure the cause of all mankind."[9] The American ideals of freedom, like those of other revolutions, had a strong transforming and, therefore, precisely because of this (and from the beginning), expansionist impetus—an impetus that, it seems to me, has not spent itself either in time or space, even if it has changed its appearance and meaning. When Thomas Jefferson spoke of an "empire for liberty," he envisioned an extended continental republic in North America. But as early as 1871, Walt Whitman envisaged a radical democracy projected beyond the continent, across the oceans, toward world supremacy:

> The Pacific will be ours, and the Atlantic mainly ours. There will be daily electric communication with every part of the globe. What an age! what

> a land! Where, elsewhere, one so great? The individuality of one nation must then, as always, lead the world. Can there be any doubt who the leader ought to be?[10]

The totem of freedom is also multifaceted. The idea of an American empire has, historically, been linked to the perpetuation of freedom in the country, to its extension abroad, and consequently and in stark contrast to this concept, to nationalist policies of standardization, dominance, and supremacy. The idea of freedom, on the other hand, has continually been the object of a multiplicity of concurrent interpretations. In the name of freedom, a whole series of conflicting trends have been justified: marked discrimination on the grounds of race, wealth, and gender, as well as dramatic struggles for emancipation; the demands of the free market and those of social security; patriotic consensus and the repression of dissidents, as well as the right to espouse dissidence. In the name of freedom, criticism has been directed at imperial policies and, sometimes, at the idea of empire itself.[11] The flag born during the American Revolution has accompanied all the many subsequent developments of that revolution. It has been, like the French *Tricouleur*, a banner of white freedom and Black slavery that could morph into a banner of Black freedom or rebellion. It has even become the emblem of groups of Americans who believe, in exactly the same way as the most heretical followers of the Red banner, that "their" flag expresses some original ideals different from those realized under the official flag—ideals that have been betrayed and of which they, instead, are the authentic custodians. These groups demand that the Stars and Stripes should represent the United States not as it is but as it should, and still has to, become. Hence, they oppose the established totem, sometimes through shocking demonstrations of contempt, but they do so to appropriate it and restore its purity. The flag is a vital and living symbol, which has solid roots in society. Precisely on account of this status, it does not have just one meaning. On the contrary, its meanings can be and, in effect, are diverse, even conflicting. They have been the terrain of social and political clashes and, consequently, of judicial disputes; and they still are (as I discuss in part 4). Precisely because of this characteristic, the symbol is so powerful.

The Stars and Stripes, whatever it represents, is a bloodthirsty totem. Like all totems, it legitimizes the killing of the enemy, but it also demands and receives the blood of its followers and ultimately symbolizes it. It is the incarnation of the secret pact that unites the members of the group in a relationship of intimate solidarity, a secret pact based on the blood that has been shed and on the accepted death of some members of the group, on the ritualized remembrance of this sacrifice aimed at the survival of the group itself and of its values, on the continuity and communion between the living and the dead. This idea of the flag holds true inasmuch as the flag is a national banner, for the wars and imperial aspirations to which it has lent its colors; and also in this regard, as is obvious, the United States is in no way an exception compared to other countries.[12] As in other countries, the sacralization of the national emblem, its transformation from an instrument for designating territory into an object of veneration, is tied to warfare. It emerged with the massacres of the Civil War and the cult of their remembrance at the end of the nineteenth century, when sacrifice and the nation-state and its symbols became inextricably interwined;[13] and it was heightened by the First and Second World Wars. It was at the beginning of the Civil War, in April 1861, in New York City, that there was the first great popular demonstration (of emotion, mourning, grief, and anger) centered around a flag fetish: the flag of Fort Sumter, which had escaped the Southern cannon shots. It was during the Civil War that the mystical reverence for the patriot-martyr developed: the soldier who, in battle, inspired by the flag, performs heroic and foolhardy acts while going knowingly toward death—and who achieves posthumous fame in poems, songs, pictures. It was then that Walt Whitman sang of the flag:

> O you up there! O pennant! where you undulate like a snake
> hissing so curious,
> Out of reach, an idea only, yet furiously fought for, risking
> bloody death, loved by me,

Blood and sanctification
The assassination of Abraham Lincoln, 1865. From left to right: Henry Rathbone, Clara Harris, Mary Todd Lincoln, Abraham Lincoln, and John Wilkes Booth. Currier & Ives, 1865. Lithograph. (Prints and Photographs Division, Library of Congress)

Blood and sanctification
Martin Luther King, 1968. “Somebody Paid the Price for Your Right: Register/Vote,” poster, A. Philip Randolph Educational Fund, ca. 1968. (Gary Yanker Collection, Prints and Photographs Division, Library of Congress)

So loved—O you banner leading the day with stars brought
from the night!
Valueless, object of eyes, over all and demanding
all—(absolute owner of all)—O banner and pennant!
I too leave the rest—great as it is, it is nothing—houses,
machines are nothing—I see them not,
I see but you, O warlike pennant! O banner so broad, with
stripes, sing you only,
Flapping up there in the wind.[14]

But it is not only the totem of armies that evokes the mesh of love and death. It is also the devotees of the liberty flag, in the United States as elsewhere, who have not refrained from exalting their hero-martyrs and their blood-drenched banners. Blood sacrifice at the border, under the national colors, may well be the holiest ritual of the nation-state; but blood sacrifice in the *maquis* or in the street, under the colors of freedom, is the holiest ritual of the freedom fighter. On the morrow of the Revolution, Jefferson recalled, with a slightly gory nonchalance, that "the tree of liberty must be refreshed from time to time with the blood of patriots & tyrants. It is it's natural manure." And that was not a mannered recollection, because it served to criticize the policy of the postrevolutionary ruling class in the face of Daniel Shays's insurrection, namely, the new popular insurrections against yesterday's insurgents, who had by now become the establishment. On the eve of the Civil War, John Brown repeated his favorite biblical quotation, "without shedding of blood there is no remission of sin," and he shed the blood of others and ultimately his own, even before the great carnage had begun.[15] After the Civil War, Frederick Douglass recalled "the heroic deeds and virtues of the brave men who volunteered, fought and fell in the cause of Union and freedom." And that was not a mannered recollection, because Douglass intended to rescue the memory of the war and of its valid reasons (the struggle against racial slavery) from the quagmire of the ongoing national reconciliation. In the name of pacification, he said, "we must not be asked to say that the South was right in the rebellion, or to say the North was wrong." And again: "We must not be asked to put no difference between those who fought for the Union and those who fought against it, or between loyalty and treason."[16] With a giant leap in time, to the end of the 1900s, a poster that invites citizens (Black citizens in particular) to register and vote carries a picture of Martin Luther King, Jr., and the assertion, "Somebody paid the price for your right." The martyred King is embraced by the Stars and Stripes as is Lincoln, in so many nineteenth-century prints, in the supreme moment of his martyrdom.[17]

Finally, the Stars and Stripes is a totem thirsty *tout court*, thirsty for alcohol, or at least it was, for a long time, in the past (and I do not know if this is an American peculiarity or exception, but I doubt it). The flag has presided over popular festivities in which, in its name, the good citizens of the republic indulged in copious drinking sessions. Mark Twain refers to this scenario, in his narration of an episode he witnessed in the West, during the Civil War. The story, recounted in an irreverent tone, is the account of a miraculous apparition of the flag and of an unrealized Bacchic celebration.[18] In a small city in Nevada, a summer storm breaks, the overhanging mountain is enveloped by dense black clouds, attracting the attention of the people. While they are all looking upward, an extraordinary thing happens. On the summit, a golden flame seems to light up, small but very bright against the dark and stormy background.

> It was the flag!—though no one suspected it at first, it seemed so like a supernatural visitor of some kind—a mysterious messenger of good tidings, some were fain to believe. It was the nation's emblem transfigured by the departing rays of a sun that was entirely palled from view. . . . The superstition grew apace that this was a mystic courier come with great news from the war—the poetry of the idea excusing and commending it—and on it spread, from heart to heart, from lip to lip and from street to street, till there was a general impulse to have out the military and welcome the bright waif with a salvo of artillery!

In fact, there really is some news: it is the day that witnesses two great Union victories of 1863, Vicksburg and Gettysburg; but no one knows it yet. If only we had known, concludes Mark Twain,

> the glorified flag . . . would have been saluted and re-saluted, that memorable evening, as long as there was a charge of powder to thunder with; the city would have been illuminated, and every man that had any respect for himself would have got drunk,—as it was the custom of the country on all occasions of public moment. Even at this distant day I cannot think of this needlessly marred supreme opportunity without regret. What a time we might have had!

The American, French, and Red flags represent three revolutionary promises that, although developed in different directions, thoroughly interacted. The socialist Red flag has been an antagonist to the liberal and democratic French and American ones. When it became a state emblem, in the Soviet Union and elsewhere, its antagonism was played out in the fields of international relations and state power politics. But before that, when it was growing into a transnational symbol of social protest, such antagonism cut across the national societies of France and the United States, with seemingly different historical results. It was in France that the confrontation took its earliest, most dramatic form. In 1848, and again in 1871, the Red banner challenged the republican *bleu-blanc-rouge* in the streets of Paris, in highly symbolic clashes between the colors of the 1789 bourgeois revolution and those of an anticipated proletarian revolution. In a famous painting, the poet and moderate republican Alphonse de Lamartine is shown in front of the Hôtel de Ville on February, 25, 1848, while rejecting with a grand gesture the Red flag in favor of the *Tricouleur*.[19] The rejection did work for the time being, but it did not prevent the *drapeau rouge* from remaining the rallying point of worker unrest, class struggle, and Socialist party politics for the rest of the nineteenth century and most of the next. In the United States, on the other hand, the symbolic confrontation knew less dramatic events but had the most radical outcome. Since the beginning of industrialization and the explosion of the Social

Question, the Red flag was marginalized, and industrial workers asserted their rights, mainly, by flying the Stars and Stripes and by joining non-socialist, multiclass parties. It was indeed a difference not just between France and the United States but, rather, it seemed, between the United States and the rest of the Western world—a truly American peculiarity. In the course of the twentieth century, generations of startled observers pondered over the quintessential exceptionalist question, Werner Sombart's "Why is there no Socialism in the United States?" and its implied generalization, "Is America substancially different?" Looking back from the vantage point of the early twenty-first century, when Socialism as a radical working-class movement has all but disappeared in the West, one may come to a somewhat divergent conclusion: perhaps the early demise of the Red flag as the powerful symbol of a social cleavage in the nation was an American peculiarity only in timing, not in substance.[20]

I Worship *The Invention of a Tradition*

Revolutionary flags on the march
Archibald M. Willard, *The Spirit of '76*, 1876. Originally entitled *Yankee Doodle*, this is one of several versions of a scene painted by A. M. Willard that came to be known as *The Spirit of '76*. Chromolithograph. (Prints and Photographs Division, Library of Congress)

Revolutionary flags on the march
Eugène Delacroix, *La Liberté guidant le peuple*, 1830. Oil on canvas. (Musée du Louvre, Paris)

1 The Spirit of '76

In 1876, the United States celebrated the first centenary of its independence with a great international exhibition in Philadelphia, a city consecrated to the Declaration of 1776 and to the Constitution. The most famous icon of that year is the picture *The Spirit of '76*, painted by Archibald M. Willard for that exhibition and then reproduced and sold in hundreds of thousands of chromolithographs. *The Spirit of '76* is reminiscent of the much more famous *La Liberté guidant le peuple* (1830), by the Frenchman Eugène Delacroix, the painting about the Parisian insurrection of July 1830, in which Liberty is an austere and attractive woman, with a Phrygian cap, who, bare-breasted and holding the *bleu-blanc-rouge* tricolor, stands on the barricades. Willard's work is less powerful, and the allegory of the revolutionary masses it proposes is trite, with a hackneyed martial air, more chaste and decidedly completely masculine. A mature veteran, a young drummer, and a piper, wounded and bandaged, march resolutely at the head of armed militiamen; behind them flutters the national flag as it should have been at the time of independence, with thirteen stripes, seven red and six white, and thirteen five-pointed white stars, arranged in a circle against a blue background, indicating the thirteen former colonies united in the revolt. In fact, that flag did not yet exist in 1776. And it certainly did not exist in April 1775, at the time of the battle of Concord, the first serious military clash of the Revolution, the battle that was commemorated in 1875, when the verses of Ralph Waldo Emerson were sculpted in stone:

> By the rude bridge that arched the flood,
> Their flag to April's breeze unfurled,
> Here, once, the embattled farmers stood,
> And fired the shot heard round the world.[1]

Whatever my imagination may have to say about this description, not even the flag of Emerson's revolutionary farmers is the Stars and Stripes.

In the early period of the Revolution, the flags were others and of various types.[2] Some were ribald and insolent; they displayed the tree of liberty or phrases such as "Liberty or death" on cloths of different colors. They often presented a rattlesnake, with thirteen rattles, menacing and ready to strike, positioned diagonally and sometimes with the words "Don't Tread on Me." The rattlesnake had been used on various occasions to represent the colonies and had all the characteristics dear to the revolutionaries: it is an animal indigenous to the Americas, it does not attack unless provoked, it warns before striking, but in the end, it is pitiless, deadly.[3] Other flags were more restrained, such as the one hoisted by the Continental Army of General George Washington in January 1776, in Boston, which was occupied by the British. It was a few months prior to independence, but independence had not yet been decided on or even completely thought through as an ultimate aim; and so Washington's flag showed thirteen red and white stripes, symbolizing colonial unity, and, in a framed section, the crosses of the British Union Jack, symbolizing permanence within the empire and loyalty to the crown. After July 4, things changed. However, at least a year had to pass before the white stars, against a blue background—flown as an autonomous flag on various occasions—were added to the red and white stripes. The new design was approved on June 14, 1777, by the Continental Congress or, rather, by one of its committees, and even then few people really noticed it. The committee that concerned itself with this issue was the Marine Committee, and it was the appropriate body to do so. In fact, even though flags were employed by land armies, they were much more important for the fleets operating in the open waters of the oceans. It had been at sea that the use of standardized flags, identifiable from afar, had become established practice in the course of the preceding centuries. And it had been the seafaring people of the new United States who had asked for a flag.

It was, therefore, the Marine Committee of Congress that voted the following resolution: "That the flag of the thirteen United States be thirteen stripes of alternate red and white; that the union be thirteen stars, white in a blue field, representing a new constellation"—a new constellation, one would imagine, in the firmament of nations. The congressional resolution does not give any reason as to the colors chosen or the arrangement of the stars. A few years later, in 1782, Congress wanted to attribute some high-flown significance to the white, red, and blue, when it employed them in the design of the Great Seal of the United States, the one with the eagle and the dictum "E Pluribus Unum": the white, it was said, signified purity and innocence; the red, vigor and valor; the blue, vigilance, perseverance, and justice.[4] In reality, the colors were adopted because they were familiar, because the fabrics and the dyes were available, because, in short, they were the colors of the British flag. As regards the arrangement of the stars, there was the greatest latitude. In some flags, the stars are arranged in a circle, sometimes in a circle of twelve stars with the thirteenth in the center. In others, the stars are arranged on several horizontal lines. In some rare instances, they constitute a bigger star. In various historical paintings that depict decisive battles of the Revolutionary War—for example, in those of the painter John Trumbull—the twelve stars are arranged in a rectangular pattern, with the thirteenth in the center, and they are six-pointed stars. In the paintings dealing with similar subjects by Charles Willson Peale, General Washington is sometimes shown with a blue flag with the stars in a circle (no stripes), sometimes with the complete Stars and Stripes. Both Trumbull and Peale were artist-revolutionaries: they had witnessed the battles that they later painted. They recorded on canvas the creative confusions of their times, when fundamental symbols were been shaped and not yet standardized.

There is an image of the flag in a famous short story by Washington Irving, "Rip Van Winkle" (1819), and it is also auroral, barely traced. In order to describe the significance and rapidity of the changes wrought by the Revolution, Irving recounts that his hero, Rip Van Winkle, wanting to get away from his despotic wife, flees to the woods, falls asleep under a tree, and wakes up twenty years later. In the meantime, of course, the Revolution has taken place. Rip is astounded. He does not understand.

He remembers a sleepy village, an inn full of layabouts, a group of friends who used to meet to read old newspapers that reported old news. Now the village is big and chaotic; the character of the people has changed. "There was a busy, bustling, disputatious tone about it, instead of the accustomed phlegm and drowsy tranquillity." Instead of the friends of earlier times, "a lean, bilious-looking fellow, with his pockets full of handbills, was haranguing vehemently about rights of citizens—elections—members of congress—liberty—Bunker's Hill—heroes of seventy-six." The portrait of King George has changed into that of another George, General Washington. In place of the big tree that shaded the peaceful inn, "there now was reared a tall, naked pole, with something on the top that looked like a red nightcap, and from it was fluttering a flag, on which was a singular assemblage of stars and stripes—all this was strange and incomprehensible." In fact, at least two comprehensible things emerge before the story ends. When Rip is asked for whom he would have voted, he replies that he is "a loyal subject of the king, God bless him!" and he almost gets thrashed: he should now be a loyal citizen of a republic. Moreover, Rip comes to know that his wife is dead: also for him, therefore, the revolutionary flag has brought the only freedom that he really cares about, freedom from the despotism of "petticoat government."[5]

In effect, no one knows with certainty when the Stars and Stripes was designed, or by whom, or when it was displayed for the first time. A convenient legend makes up for this lack of knowledge. The core of the legend is that the original flag was conceived and made a few days before the Declaration of Independence—therefore, the flag precedes and accompanies the birth of the nation—and that it was made by a Philadelphia upholsterer and seamstress, Elisabeth Griscom Ross, known as Betsy Ross, at the request of General Washington: the father of the nation and of the flag is, therefore, finally accompanied by a mother. I say finally because it was only after the Civil War, almost a century after the events, that this woman-centered episode (which clashes ironically with the antimatriarchal allusions of Irving's story) was revealed by one of Betsy's grandsons. Until then it had been unknown, and afterward historians did all they could to try and find proofs and confirmation, but without succeeding. The grandson, William J. Canby, said that he had heard this story from his grandmother herself and from the other women of the family, and he tried to lend it scientific authoritativeness, incorporating it in a paper he read before the Pennsylvania Historical Society in 1870.[6] This paper is a curious text. Entitled "The History of the Flag of the United States," it begins as if it were a historical critical study conducted with all the tools and circumspections of the historian's trade. An account is given of the research carried out in libraries and archives and of the frustrating results of this research. The official record, says Canby, confirms the scant information already known; it is "bare and unsatisfying, involved in a mass of conjecture, with but one central point": the resolution of the committee of the Continental Congress of June 14, 1777, which I have already mentioned. That is all.

Canby, however, does not admit defeat. Faced with the silence of the written sources, he says, the historian can turn to tradition, which is not only "a pleasing kind of romance," an invention without foundation; when one can talk to the people who have known the protagonists of history, "tradition, uncontradicted by the written record, stands unimpeachable, quite as reliable and often more so, than the books." At this point, the tone of the text changes. The language and structure of the scientific study are replaced by those of, precisely, the romance—namely, the sentimental novels of love and marriage and death, of domestic and civic life, generally woman-centered and written almost exclusively by women for women, novels that then enjoyed great popularity and commercial success. When Canby announces that, according to a well-known tradition in the family, "this lady is the one to whom belongs the honor of having made with her own hands the first flag," he initiates a narration that throws to the wind any critical circumspection. From that point on, carried on the flow of memory, his characters think and speak in quotation marks (their innermost thoughts are revealed), their happenings are full of details and dramatic events, and Betsy is characterized as an exemplary woman. Betsy Griscom, the daughter of an influential Quaker carpenter, is prudent and industrious; she never wastes her time chatting or in the street and so is greatly respected by her neighbors. She is of an independent spirit and since she was a girl has been an apprentice upholsterer. She marries her workmate John Ross, with whom she opens a small workshop. John dies almost immediately, leaving the young widow in difficulty, in the hard times of the Revolutionary War. Betsy, states Canby, "often pondered over the future, and brooded sometimes almost to despondency upon her troubles, yet she always rallied when she reflected upon the goodness of Providence who had never deserted her."

Providence materializes in the bodies of certain gentlemen who, on a day in June 1776, enter her shop. One of these gentlemen is Colonel George Ross, her late husband's uncle and a Pennsylvania delegate of the Continental Congress, which held its meetings not far from there. Betsy recognizes, in another gentleman, "the handsome form and features of the dignified, yet graceful and polite Commander in Chief, who, while he was yet Colonel Washington had visited her shop both professionally and socially many times." According to the account given by Betsy's daughter, the financier Robert Morris was also present. The men introduce themselves as members of a congressional committee charged with preparing a flag (even though, in fact, Washington was not a member of the Congress) and ask Betsy to make it. They present sketches and drawings, which Betsy, in her sitting room, discusses and revises with General Washington. Her main suggestion concerns the stars: they should have not six points but five. They tell her that she is right but that five-pointed stars are difficult to make. There is nothing easier, she replies, and shows them how it is done. After a few days' work, the first flag is ready. It is presented to Congress and approved. Betsy is given the task of producing the flags in great numbers for the government, an enterprise to which she will dedicate the rest of her life—an intense life, in which she will display many virtues, not only business ability but also her commitment to charitable works, caring for the sick and preparing medicinal potions. In her old age, she becomes, for her neighbors, "like a kind shepherdess amidst her sheep, looked up to and beloved by all."

Adoration Charles H. Weisgerber, *Birth of Our Nation's Flag*, 1893. Oil on canvas. (Courtesy of the State Museum of Pennsylvania, Pennsylvania Historical and Museum Commission)

Adoration Hieronymus Bosch, *The Epiphany*, or *The Adoration of the Magi* (c. 1495). Detail of center panel of triptych, oil on wood panels. (John G. Johnson Collection, Philadelphia Museum of Art)

But the romance is not finished yet. Canby is still not satisfied. Betsy, after having married Captain Joseph Ashbourne, of the American Merchant Navy, is once again widowed. Captain Ashbourne is in fact captured by the British (events are still unfolding during the Revolution) and sent to the prisons of Plymouth, in England, which were notorious for the horrid conditions of their underground cells, where gentlemen of the best families, merchants, officers, and ordinary soldiers suffered indiscriminate death because of the contagious diseases and fever generated by the nauseating and infected air. There Ashbourne languishes and dies, but not before having been cared for and comforted by a fellow prisoner, named John Claypoole, to whom he also entrusts his last messages of love for Betsy. Claypoole, Canby recounts, "strange to say . . . had been a former lover of the youthful Betsy Griscom"; having been freed and having returned to his country at the end of the war, he visits the widow, reevokes the circumstances of their former intimacy, and marries her. Betsy Ross is, therefore, at the center of a whirl of family names: Elizabeth Griscom as an unmarried girl, then Ross, then Elizabeth Ashbourne, and finally Elizabeth Claypoole and the widow Claypoole in the very last years of her long life—a whirl of names, marriages, and widowhood that was not at all unusual for the times. The woman really existed: she was born in 1752 and died in 1836 at the age of eighty-four, and she was also really a flag maker by profession, a fact documented at least since 1777. As for the rest, who knows? In any case, true or not, after 1870 it all became a well-known story. And Willard could include the Stars and Stripes in *The Spirit of '76* without having too many philological scruples about it.

Just over twenty years after the revelation of the story of Betsy Ross, it was immortalized in a painting by Charles H. Weisgerber, *Birth of Our Nation's Flag* (1893). The painting was done, exactly as with Willard's *The Spirit of '76*, in order to be displayed at an international exhibition, the Columbian Exposition of 1893, which, with a year's delay, celebrated in Chicago the fifth centenary of the European discovery of America. There the painting was hailed as a strong touch of national symbolism. At the same time, Weisgerber launched a fund-raising campaign to buy what was considered to be Betsy Ross's house in Philadelphia and to turn it into a museum and a patriotic shrine. With this aim in mind, in 1898 he was involved in founding the American Flag House and Betsy Ross Memorial Association. Each of the approximately two million contributors received a certificate that included a color reproduction of the 1893 painting, which thus became very popular, invaded domestic spaces and public buildings, and was reproduced in school and history books. In spite of some suspicions about financial scandals and embezzlement, the Betsy Ross Memorial Association succeeded in its aim; in 1937, the Betsy Ross House was made over to the city of Philadelphia, and it is, to this day, one of the most frequented tourist sites in the city. But the original canvas of *Birth of Our Nation's Flag* remained the property of the artist's heirs, and throughout the second half of the twentieth century, it was kept rolled up, far from the public gaze. Finally, it was restored and donated to the State Museum of Pennsylvania in Harrisburg. Before that, it was exhibited at the 2000 Republican National Convention in Philadelphia, the one that triumphally chose George W. Bush as a presidential candidate.

The style of Weisgerber's painting is austere, faux archaic in the rigid and frozen gestures of the figures. The composition of the painting shows the humble seamstress holding the flag (with the thirteen stars arranged in a circle) on her knees and showing it to General George Washington, who, in uniform, sits solemnly facing her. The general is flanked by George Ross and Robert Morris, who, however, are not involved in the intense and intimate rapport between Washington and Betsy. The dressmaker's instruments and the pieces of cloth scattered everywhere indicate that the work has just been completed. A limpid ray of sunshine descends from the window to illuminate the scene and imbue it with a mystical aura. The iconographic reminiscences recall the Nativity of Christ or the Adoration of the Magi, perhaps a Hieronymus Bosch *Epiphany*. Here, Betsy Ross is a Madonna, the hallowed mother of the flag and the nation, born from her womb after her mysterious "encounter" with the *primus inter pares* of the Founding Fathers, Washington himself. She is, in effect, the Founding Mother, the incarnation of the ideal of the republican mother of nineteenth-century culture—a woman devoted to her duty of caring for others in the family and community spheres (as I have already mentioned, Betsy is an exemplary wife and mother, as well as a benefactress of her neighbors), who, precisely because of this role, contributes to founding the civic values of the republic. The fact that, after having conceived the flag, Betsy becomes a capable entrepreneur and succeeds in the male sphere of the market seems to vanish. And the flag in Weisgerber's painting appears more domestic and feminine than the martial, masculine one envisioned by Willard in 1876, but it is so only in appearance: it is still the fruit of a woman's body offered to a warrior chief, a male combatant.[7]

Betsy Ross became the only heroine in an entirely male national pantheon of heroes. She was claimed by conservative women's organizations and later by proto-feminist groups.[8] And today she is, ironically, for many students, by far the best-known "historical" figure of American history—after presidents, statesmen, and generals.[9] Above all, at the end of the nineteenth century, her legend was absorbed in the renewed and more widespread cult of the flag that was establishing itself in society. Throughout the first half of the nineteenth century, the Stars and Stripes had had a relatively weak presence in the country's cultural landscape. Of course, it was the flag of the Independence and Revolutionary War, as well as, one would add with the benefit of hindsight, the first national flag in the modern sense of the term. In fact, until the revolutions of the late eighteenth century, flags did not represent peoples or nations but rather sovereigns and ruling families, whose coat of arms would be at the center of the flags, which would be associated with armies and fleets, fluttering on forts and ships. The British Union Jack itself is the synthesis of the symbols of the united monarchies of England and Scotland and, later, of Ireland; it was known as "the King's colours" and was a naval standard (that is what *jack* means). Things changed after the revolutions. The Stars and Stripes, like the slightly later French tricolor, was a republican and national flag, egalitarian, without a symbolic monarchical center to which to pay homage, and it was intended for everyone. Nevertheless, at least in American society, it took many years and, finally, another revolutionary war, the Civil War, before the flag could truly become a symbol of popular identity and enter, so to speak, into people's homes as a familiar presence—as a revered piece of fabric, as the main character of pious patriotic narratives, as the bright central focus of a Weisgerber or Willard print.

2 New Cults for Old Glory

The popular cult of the Stars and Stripes developed slowly. In the first decades of the Republic, the flag was to be found in the paintings of revolutionary artists such as Trumbull and Peale or in the most famous one by the German American Emmanuel Gottlieb Leutze, *Washington Crossing the Delaware* (1851), which was painted in Germany. The flag appeared in prints and scarves next to symbols of the revolutionary period such as busts of Washington, eagles and seals of the Republic, liberty goddesses and freedom trees, Phrygian caps (the "red nightcap" that impresses Rip Van Winkle). More mundanely, it decorated plates, crockery, and glassware with designs of ships decked with flags. However, in everyday life, it continued to be associated with naval, military, and political institutions. The widespread diffusion of the Stars and Stripes began to emerge in the celebrations of the national holiday, the Fourth of July, and then in electoral campaigns. The presidential election of 1840 between the Democrat Martin Van Buren, the incumbent president, and the challenger, William H. Harrison of the Whig Party, marked a decisive turning point in this direction, a turning point not necessarily for the better. Harrison presented himself as a rude frontier pioneer, used to living in a log cabin, and attacked Van Buren by depicting him as an effeminate dandy, unworthy of the virile, full-blooded American democracy. In rallies and demonstrations, the Whig canvassers reinforced the sexual innuendos with intense flag-waving, in an unprecedented manner. The message was clear: Harrison was a real he-man American, and his adversary was a lesser being. The tactic worked, even if Harrison paid dearly for the macho style he had adopted. Elected president, he refused to wear an overcoat at the swearing-in ceremony, in the open air on a very cold day. He caught pneumonia and died a few days later.[1]

The first real outburst of mass enthusiasm for the flag broke out in the north of the country in spring 1861, following the secession of the

Southern slave states. The northern cities and countryside were swept by a wave of patriotism and outrage at the breakup of the Union, and they covered themselves in the national colors. For the first time, the national colors fluttered not only from ships, barracks, and public buildings but also from hotels and shops, colleges and schools, rooftops and balconies, and finally, churches; flags were associated with the cross and the name of God and became a kind of domestic idol in every family. In many cases, it was difficult *not* to wave them; otherwise one could be suspected of treason. There was also a commercial boom. The demand for flags was so great that the manufacturers could not meet it; stocks ran out, and prices rocketed. In the South, naturally, the Stars and Stripes was taken down (a member of the federal Cabinet ordered the immediate execution, by firing squad, of anyone who did so, but it was more of a hysterical reaction than a concrete proposal) and was replaced by the flag of the newly born Confederate States of America. That flag had three horizontal bands, two red and a central white one, and a blue corner with seven white stars, which later became eleven and finally thirteen, to indicate the member states. In effect, the rebel flag, known as the Stars and Bars, resembled too closely the one that had just been repudiated. On the battlefield, it was difficult to distinguish from the enemy's flag: the soldiers did not know whom to shoot at. Therefore, the Confederate government adopted a different combat standard, a blue cross of St. Andrew with the white stars set in a red background—the Southern Cross. And in 1863, it was incorporated in a new national flag, in which it occupied the top left-hand corner; the rest of the cloth was a sinister immaculate white—"the Stainless Banner," it was called, "the White man's flag." It was, nevertheless, the Southern Cross that was remembered as the flag of the South.[2]

Throughout the war, the Stars and Stripes remained the flag of the United States of America, that is, in fact, of the Unionist North. But in the minds of the Unionists, it remained also the flag of the entire nation "one and indivisible," not divisible certainly by a secession considered an impossibility according to Constitution, history, and logic. President Abraham Lincoln insisted, among other things, that the number of stars should be kept at thirty-four, not recognizing the breakaway of the Confederate States. The star-spangled banner, like the idea of nationhood, acquired then an unheard-of pathos in the speeches and experiences of the Northern elite and of ordinary citizens, millions of whom fought under that standard in vast armies and under it died by the hundreds of thousands. At war's end, it was under the colors of the Stars and Stripes that the oath of allegiance was taken by the repentant rebels who asked to be readmitted in the national community. And it was repeated in a thousand ways that the nation's territorial, political, and historical identity had been ratified by the blood of its sons, as well as by the blood of the noble father Lincoln, murdered in a theater box decorated with flags. The assassination occurred on April 14, 1865, Good Friday, and the president-martyr was likened by many people to the figure of Christ. The box flag decorations did not succeed in protecting the man from martyrdom, but they succeeded in punishing his assassin, the actor John Wilkes Booth. Booth, after the misdeed, escaped by jumping onto the stage below, but his foot got caught in a Stars and Stripes festoon, and he fell and fractured his femur. That made his escape slow and exhausting and eventually facilitated his capture.[3]

With the Civil War, the national flag established itself as the central, pervasive icon of Northern public life. It also acquired the name of Old Glory, which it retains to this day. The account of how that name became popular tells the story of the transformation of a prewar, commercial, naval flag into a symbol of patriotism during the war—a very personal, domestic patriotism. In 1824, Captain William Driver, the commander of the brigantine *Charles Doggett,* based at Salem, Massachusetts, becomes the proud owner of a flag that accompanies him, for years, on the world's trade routes. Driver retires and goes to live in Nashville, Tennessee, where he adopts the habit, on public holidays, of displaying the flag that he has by now affectionately named Old Glory. When, in 1861, Tennessee secedes from the Union, the rebels look for the flag in order to destroy it, but they cannot find it. The captain, a loyal Unionist, has hidden it well, having had it sewn inside a quilt (the duvet on his bed). He brings it out only when the Union troops liberate Nashville in 1862; and it is he himself who hoists it above the dome of the city's capitol, as it is greeted by the soldiers' hurrahs. Thus, Old Glory became a public legend, the most famous of many similar legends of Stars-and-Stripes flags hidden and saved in the South by Unionist sympathizers—even if, generally, the protagonists of these episodes are not rough sailors but housewives. In 1922, Captain Driver's heirs donated the old flag to the Smithsonian Institution in Washington, D.C., where it is kept to this day. I like to recall, however, the folksy tale according to which the Smithsonian flag is a fake, the original having been eaten by a mule a long time ago.

After the Civil War, public flag celebrations acquired intensity, passion, and a baroque taste for formality.[4] Some of these formalities were not new but were renewed and strengthened, such as those associated with the Fourth of July, Independence Day. In the first decades of the Republic, "the glorious Fourth" was often a partisan and party event. Federalists and Republicans, Whigs and Democrats remembered the Revolution, making the most of their own specific and contrasting interpretations of the revolutionary heritage. In some instances, the celebrations had ended in a brawl. There were often demonstrations on the part of antislavery activists, trade unionists, or suffragists who laid claim to the promise of equality of the Declaration of Independence, a promise that had not been kept. Even when political controversies did not flare up, the festivities were popular, noisy, exuberant, chaotic. The flag presided over parades, music, street shows, picnics, fireworks displays, and big drinking sessions (those nostalgically recalled by Mark Twain)—as well as the incidents resulting from the enthusiastic abuse of alcohol and fireworks.[5] The middle-class citizens were shocked by this activity and spoke with disgust not of a "glorious Fourth" but rather of a "barbarous Fourth," vulgar and dangerous. And after the Civil War, they went to a lot of trouble to reform it, to make it safe and respectable, less controversial and less partisan, more patriotic and national, and finally to put it under the control of the authorities. At the beginning of the twentieth century, the attempts at reform had achieved some success, even if its promoters were not completely satisfied. In fact, the most well-to-do Americans avoided the Fourth of July ceremonies, leaving them to the populace, whether native or immigrant.

In a 1905 pamphlet, a party boss from Manhattan, George Washington Plunkitt, described this estrangement with insolent—although fairly accurate—cynicism. His organization was the famous Tammany Hall, the Irish- and immigrant-dominated Democratic electoral machine that was, according to him, the sworn enemy of the old urban elites who boasted parted-in-the-middle surnames going back to the revolutionary era. (The son-of-Ireland Plunkitt has only the weighty double given name, George Washington.) "Nobody pays any attention to the Fourth of July any longer, except Tammany and the small boy," said Plunkitt. When the glorious day arrives, the "aristocrats" of the silk-stocking districts rush to their country homes. They want to avoid the confusion. "They don't want to be annoyed with firecrackers and the Declaration of Independence"; they do not want to mix with common people. They behave like his dog, which, every year, for fear of fireworks, disappears in the woods of the Bronx on the eve of the Fourth and returns home forty-eight hours later, as precisely as a clock. The popular Tammany is, in contrast, the most patriotic organization on earth; it has a real love of the Stars and Stripes.

> Did you ever see Tammany Hall decorated for a celebration? It's just a mass of flags. They even take down the window shades and put flags in place of them. There's flags everywhere except on the floors. We don't care for expense where the American flag is concerned, especially after we have won an election.

After an election victory, concluded Plunkitt, they controlled the municipal funds and could afford "to make an extra investment in patriotism."[6]

In the meantime, other investments in patriotism had come from different quarters and had produced truly new flag cults. After 1865, the flag display was the dominant feature of the commemorative ceremonies for the soldiers killed in battle, ceremonies that spread both in the North and the South and, at least at the outset, with different and clashing flags. The

Stars and Stripes marked Memorial Day, proclaimed by the Grand Army of the Republic (GAR), the Unionist veterans' association; inaugurated on May 30, 1868, in a few years it became a legal public holiday in all the Northern states. The Southern colors, instead, marked the Confederate Memorial Day, celebrated by the Southern veterans on various spring dates well distinct from the Yankee equivalent. The animosities between the two sides faded in time, and after 1880 the days of remembrance became opportunities for overcoming divisions and achieving national reconciliation and, therefore, opportunities to forget. There were joint ceremonies between the former enemies, the two flags began to flutter side by side, and finally the Stars and Stripes once again prevailed. It was in this climate that in 1889 Congress passed a law, after having previously dismissed it, that made May 30 the national, and not merely regional, Memorial Day. (Since 1971, and following the Monday Holiday Act of 1968, Memorial Day is the last Monday in May.) Naturally there was a price to pay. The new rhetoric of memory glorified the good faith, courage, and patriotism of all the soldiers, boys in blue and gray alike, their common idealism, their common Americanness. It ignored the reasons for the war and consequently the reasons for the divisions; thus, it made the issue of slavery disappear. Reconciliation was seen as being between white Americans—at the expense of black Americans, no longer slaves but now segregated and removed from the national consciousness.[7]

The commemorative days therefore became holidays for whites (even though many blacks protested vigorously and celebrated *their* commemorative days for *their* soldiers killed in war: almost two hundred thousand of them had served in the Union army). These commemorative days were also, from the beginning, both in the North and the South, celebrations of male military heroism. Amid the jubilation of the flags, the veterans extolled their masculinity, presented themselves as the protectors of their land, their homes, and their families, and displayed their paternal concern for widows and orphans. It was only male orators who spoke from the platforms, and it was only men who marched in the parades wrapped in patriotic colors. Women were like decorative elements: they were part of the public, or they honored the sense of duty and the sacrifice of the living males by placing flowers on the tombs of the fallen.[8] Toward the end of the nineteenth century, all this became a problem. According to many observers, the flag should take on a wider significance: it should expand and occupy new social spaces beyond the streets and the cemeteries; it should not merely be a symbol of war and, moreover, by then, of a distant war. A move in that direction came from the so-called hereditary societies, elite groups who gathered the descendants of the first settlers and who, on account of this relation, considered themselves more American than anyone else. Particularly committed in this regard were a host of women's associations, and among them the largest and best known, the Daughters of the American Revolution (DAR), founded in 1890. The DAR took under its maternal wing the domestic and feminine legend of Betsy Ross. And together with the GAR veterans, they tried to exploit to their own ends the enormous possibilities offered by the schools of the republic.[9]

The interest in schools began to appear in the 1880s. In 1885, a Wisconsin schoolmaster organized for his pupils a "day of the flag," to commemorate the anniversary of its official adoption—which occurred, as I have mentioned, on June 14, 1777. From that episode, there sprang a current of opinion that aimed at making June 14 a Flag Day to be celebrated in all the nation's educational institutions. Among the promoters of this initiative, there were daily newspapers and periodicals, teachers' associations and philanthropic societies, and of course patriotic societies and hereditary societies. After 1890, Flag Day was observed in New York and Philadelphia, Chicago and elsewhere, often with the participation of municipal and state school boards. Local authorities began to arrange that, on that day, the national flag should be displayed in public places, and they invited citizens to do likewise in their own homes. Some states ordered that the flag should always fly on school buildings, throughout the year. The students had to be actively involved in the ceremonies. There were rallies, flag-raisings, hymns and songs, inspired speeches, the waving of small individual flags. A spectacular invention was the living flag, made up of rows of children (the more there were, the better) dressed in red or white or blue and arranged to represent the Stars and Stripes in courtyards, squares, staircases.[10] There were school plays in which pupils impersonated Betsy Ross and General Washington and perhaps had to repeat the lines of a popular 1920s pageant:

> Oh!—I've lost my heart to Betsy, to Betsy, to Betsy!
>
> . . . .
>
> Oh!—Because she sewed so neatly, so neatly, so neatly![11]

Schoolgirls were advised to make flags during sewing classes, imitating the Mother of the nation.

In 1892, the most important children's periodical in the country, Boston's *The Youth's Companion*, launched a campaign to publicize in schools a Pledge of Allegiance or oath of loyalty to the flag, prepared by its editorial office. The magazine had a circulation of half a million copies and, to advertise itself, had already undertaken various patriotic promotional activities; it was now looking for a way to increase sales even more, and the Pledge seemed appropriate to the purpose. The year was also appropriate. The celebrations for the fourth centenary of the European discovery of America promised to be spectacular, an opportunity not to be lost. With the blessing of the president of the United States, Benjamin Harrison, the initiative proved to be successful. On October 12, 1892, millions of pupils repeated the oath, solemnly saluting the Stars and Stripes raised by groups of veterans. Thus began a ritual that became obligatory in several states. The wording of the original Pledge (subsequently modified, as I will later explain) was, "I pledge allegiance to my flag and to the Republic for which it stands, one Nation indivisible, with liberty and justice for all." It was written by Francis C. Bellamy, a rather colorful character, a journalist who had formerly been a Baptist minister, rejected by his church because he had preached Christian socialism against the evils of capitalism; he was, among other things, a cousin of Edward Bellamy, the author of the influential utopian novel *Looking Backward* (1888), set in an America that had become socialist in the year 2000. As a Christian and a socialist, Francis Bellamy often likened the Pledge to the Lord's

Prayer, but he also thought of including in it "the historic slogan of the French Revolution which meant so much to Jefferson and his friends, 'Liberty, Equality, Fraternity.'" In the end, he deleted the French quotation, maintaining that equality and fraternity would be too controversial, too anti-individualistic for the Americans of the time. He considered the words *freedom* and *justice* to be more ecumenical, "applicable to either an individualist or a socialist state." Optimistically, he left the option open to future generations.[12]

Proponents of Flag Day and the Pledge of Allegiance had an obvious and declared goal. They aimed at the Americanization of the immigrants and social peace in the workplace; they wanted to win the minds and hearts of the sons of the newly arrived and of the proletariat in a period of marked immigration and harsh working-class conflicts, perhaps the harshest and most violent the country has ever known. On account of this goal, their preferred targets were the junior and lower secondary schools, in a system that was, by then, one of mass education. Only later were these cults incorporated into partisan political strategies—for example, in the ultra-patriotic presidential campaign conducted in 1896 by the Republicans (who tried to appropriate, outright, Flag Day and the flag)—or into the imperialistic rhetoric unleashed by the war with Spain in 1898. Among the nationalist agitators, there was the conviction, shared by their European counterparts, that nationalist sentiments were natural, primordial, and ever present, and were merely waiting to be reawakened, like the sleeping beauty, by the patriot's kiss. But there was also another conviction, namely, that the strategy of reawakening was powerless with the masses of the foreign-born who, if anything, carried with them the seeds of different loyalties. They could be excluded or assimilated; in the latter case, their Americanness had to be created from scratch. With regard to them, the patriot had to become an educator and bearer of gifts, and the Stars and Stripes was the main symbolic gift: displayed with reverence by the old owners (the Americans with a pedigree), it was given, under certain conditions, to the new owners (the immigrants) and gratefully accepted by them.

The ceremonies characterized by the donation of the flag did not arise as state initiatives but rather were initiated by individuals and organizations of the civil society. And from civil society they borrowed not only patriotism but also a surprising mix of religiosity and commercialism. The language of the flag became mystical. In the orations of the time, the Stars and Stripes was spoken of as a sacred thing, which comes from the hands of God, which the Americans should adore like the Israelites adored the Ark of the Covenant. In youth literature, the flag came to be endowed with magical or miraculous properties; it can do what the comic-book superheroes would later do: it saves children from fires and crumbling houses, it helps them to overcome obstacles, to learn arithmetic, to be successful in life. And yet the days dedicated to the celebrations became opportunities for commercial amusement and mass consumerism. This change happened above all to celebrations already well established (certainly it was not yet the case with Flag Day). The Fourth of July was and remained a day of boisterous merrymaking and carousing. The mournful Memorial Day did not remain long mournful. It became a day of dinners and balls, of amateur athletics competitions, and then, increasingly, of spectacular sporting competitions; in 1911, it became the day of the Indianapolis 500, the most popular motorcar race in the country. Both Independence Day and Memorial Day became important dates in the calendar of cut-price sales for the department stores. The Stars and Stripes appeared in storefronts and shop windows. It also appeared on the packaging and advertising of many products: cigars, beer, whiskey, cereals, biscuits, ham, various types of machines, soaps, cod-liver oil, boxer shorts, dog coats. The flag sells, said the first publicity handbooks. But then, didn't the Pledge of Allegiance itself come into being as a gadget in the advertising campaign of a high-circulation periodical?[13]

3 Flag Etiquette

Around the time of the First World War and then during and immediately after the Second, the federal government vigorously intervened, took full possession of the Stars and Stripes, and officially defined the rules for its use as well as its shape and size. It is not surprising that it was the wartime experience that encouraged these changes. As the New York intellectual Randolph Bourne wrote in 1918, "war is the health of the State" (with a capital letter). In normal times, said Bourne, the State is a vague emblem of which we are only vaguely aware during patriotic festivities; for the rest of the time, we deal with Government (with a capital letter), that is, with a fragmented set of agencies and procedures, party and personal struggles, political conflicts, controversial decisions. In wartime, however, the State is aroused: it becomes a mystical concept, a single body that mobilizes the citizens, turning them into "obedient, respectful, trustful children," and it does not tolerate dissent; free debate is replaced by coercion, love of country by reverence for the flag. And the flag becomes "solely a symbol of the political State, inseparable from its prestige and expansion"—"the banner of war."[1] Bourne was a radical, a critical spirit, a pacifist; but here he hits the mark. The Great War, which he lived through (he died at the time of the Armistice, aged thirty-two, struck down by the Spanish influenza epidemic), witnessed the explosion of a popular flagmania similar to that of the Civil War. It was a spontaneous outburst that in 1917, just as in 1861, led to producers' stocks running out and to extortionate levels in the prices of flags. Congress and President Woodrow Wilson exploited with effective entrepreneurial skill this spontaneous outburst. In their federal antisedition legislation, patterned on similar laws already existing in some states, they made insulting national symbols a criminal offense. They stood by and watched when, on various occasions, ultra-patriotic groups attacked their fellow citizens who opposed the war and forced them to kiss the flag (a piece of cloth that could have been covered with microbes, complained one of the victims, but his complaint was not well received). And they put the national colors at the service of a federal Committee on Public Information, which, headed by progressive journalist George Creel, promised to "advertise America" and "the gospel of Americanism."[2]

The Creel committee and other federal agencies used the Stars and Stripes with grand prodigality, and with all the subtlety and vulgarity of commercial advertisement, to mobilize the hearts and minds of citizens in the war effort. The propaganda-poster campaign was particularly conspicuous, perhaps more intense than in any other single belligerent country. The glossy chromaticity and sleek design of the flag highlighted public calls for recruiting soldiers for the battlefields and workers for the war industries, for conserving foods, selling government bonds, supporting charity fund drives—for "doing your bit" for the country and so proving that you are "100% American." The most famous and lasting icon of the period was the *I Want You for U.S. Army* lithograph, a portrait of Uncle Sam pointing at the viewer, distributed in millions of copies by the military authorities. But even more than the aged and slightly cartoonish Uncle Sam in a red-white-and-blue garb, it was the female figure that caught the patriotic and perhaps erotic imagination of the male artists. A beautiful woman flanked by the flag, or literally wearing it as a dress, symbolized the nation: sometimes a proud farmer with a red Phrygian cap sowing the seeds of victory, sometimes a bold classical Columbia brandishing a sword to exhort and protect, sometimes a sensuous and vulnerable America in need of manly protection ("It's Up to You! Protect the Nation's Honor. Enlist Now").[3] To defend the nation's honor, men should become crusaders, and *Pershing's Crusaders* (1918) was the title of a government-sponsored motion picture, part documentary and part fiction, the first of three official war flicks released serially under the general title *Following the Flag to France*. In the film's publicity poster, General John J. Pershing on horseback leads the American Expeditionary Force to Europe, followed by a large U.S. flag; in the background, the ghosts of medieval knights on white horses, with crosses on their oblong shields, ride along. Even in those frenzied days, such imagery raised a few eyebrows. A reviewer in the Arts and Leisure section of the *New York Times* found "something of fault" with it and wrote that the ancient crusaders represented "a system of militarism entirely out of harmony with the expressed ideals of America": the explicit linking of the Allied cause to the crusade spirit "shows a sadly deficient appreciation of the purpose of the war as set forth by President Wilson." Needless to say, the theater for the New York City opening of the movie was decorated with flags and bunting, plus a real treat: old French flags loaned by a private collector.[4]

In the meantime, the flag and some of its celebrations had been nationally standardized. Two presidential executive orders, by William Howard Taft in 1912 and Wilson in 1916, indicated precisely, and for the first time, the proportions of the design of the stars, the stripes, and the flag as a whole. The relationship between height and length of the cloth was set at 1:1.9, which gave it its definitive elongated and slender shape, different from the more square and thickset one that appears in so many nineteenth-century illustrations. The executive orders referred to the flags acquired by federal offices, which had until then, it was calculated, been supplied with no less than sixty-six different types; but they also influenced the private market. (The exact shades of the colors were defined by the government in 1934 and are known as O.G. Red and O.G. Blue, where "O.G." stands for Old Glory.) Moreover, Wilson announced that Flag Day, the fourteenth of June, would be celebrated throughout the country, every year, with a message from the president (only in 1949 did it become a national holiday by law of Congress). With appropriately lugubrious patriotic rhetoric, the announcement was full of references to death and the dead; it was made on May 30, 1916, Memorial Day, and quoted Lincoln's most famous speech, the one the martyr-president delivered at the Gettysburg War Cemetery in the fall of 1863. Wilson asked American citizens to remain united to resist the "influences which have seemed to threaten to divide us in interest and sympathy." "In the words of Abraham Lincoln," he said, "let us on [this] day rededicate ourselves to the Nation, 'one and inseparable,' from which every thought that is not worthy of our fathers' first vows . . . shall be excluded."[5]

A different type of standardization occurred after the end and in the wake the Great War, when a civilian ceremonial of the flag was developed, a flag etiquette modeled on the one already in use in the armed forces. This was done by two National Flag Conferences that met in Washington, D.C., in 1923 and 1924. Among the main promoters there was the American Legion, the veterans' organization founded in 1919; among the participants, about seventy associations in all, there were the Daughters of the American Revolution, the Women's Relief Corps, the General Federation of Women's Clubs, the Boy Scouts, the American Federation of Labor, representatives of the Army and Navy and, well, of the Ku Klux Klan. The initiative returned then to the voluntary patriotic societies, which laid down a series of rules of respect for the national flag, with which I will deal in a moment, immediately summarized in a "Flag Catechism" with ninety-six questions and answers. The White House gave its support, and President Warren Harding came to visit. In a speech to the delegates, Harding confessed to a concern, namely, that Americans barely knew the verses of "The Star-Spangled Banner," which was not yet the official national anthem (it became so only in 1931) but was already an informal "national air." He said, "I have noted audiences singing our national air—that is not the way to put it—I have noted them trying to sing our national air and outside of about 2 per cent, nearly all were mumbling their words, pretending to sing."[6] In his opinion, this was not the right way to honor the flag; it was opportune to take action, to educate people. The conferences brought a first change to the Pledge of Allegiance. The words "to my flag" were replaced with "to the flag of the United States of America," to prevent immigrants getting mixed up, in case they thought they were swearing loyalty to the national colors of their countries of origin. Americanism and fear of subversive foreign radicals indeed pervaded both conferences.

In June 1942, during the Second World War, again at the urging of patriotic organizations, the civilian flag etiquette was incorporated in a resolution of Congress approved without much scrutiny and signed into law by President Franklin D. Roosevelt. It was then that people began talking about a real Flag Code, even if its provisions had no real legal enforcing power. They were written in the conditional tense and generally did not envisage penalties for people who infringed them, except for certain acts committed in the District of Columbia, which is under direct congressional jurisdiction (specific punishments could be contemplated by specific federal or state "desecration laws," as I will show in a subsequent chapter).[7] According to the Flag Code, which is still in the books today, the flag should be displayed from sunrise to sunset and at night only if adequately illuminated for some specific patriotic effects. It should not be hung out when the weather is inclement, unless it is an all-weather flag. It should be "hoisted briskly and lowered ceremoniously" and fly every day on public buildings, schools, and polling stations. In the territory of the United States, it should always fly higher than any other banner or, on particular occasions, at the same height as other national flags; only the United Nations flag can have a preeminent position and only at the United Nations headquarters in New York. The Stars and Stripes should not lower itself or bow down in front of anyone or anything—"the undippable flag," as the novelist Kurt Vonnegut called it, maintaining that it is something that no other nation has, something that prevents friendly and respectful forms of greetings.[8] But that is not true: other countries have similar rules. It is true, however, that the U.S. team was among the first in its refusal to dip the national flag to the authorities of the nation that hosts the Olympic games, during the official ceremonies. It seems that the tradition was born at the 1908 Olympics in London, to signal censure of King Edward VII ("This flag dips for no earthly king," said the flag carrier, according to a dubious story), or perhaps, more consistently, at the 1936 Olympics in Berlin to signal censure of Adolf Hitler's Nazi regime.[9]

It is fortunate that the provisions of the federal Flag Code are not really legally binding because, otherwise, millions of Americans would be in trouble. The provisions are indeed very punctilious and are sometimes at variance with popular usage. The flag, in fact, should not touch anything beneath it, the floor or the ground or water or merchandise, but always flutter freely in the wind. It should not be carried horizontally or upside down, with the stars pointing downward. It should not be used to cover a ceiling. It should not be draped on the roof or on the back of vehicles, on railway carriages or boats. It should not have symbols, drawings, or words unrelated to its original design; nor should it be reproduced on clothing, curtains, sheets, pillows, or any kind of advertising. Still less should it be printed on disposable products such as paper handkerchiefs or cardboard boxes. It can be worn as a brooch or pin on the left lapel near the heart. The flag, it is said, "represents a living country and is itself considered a living thing." The 1942 Flag Code also included the Pledge of Allegiance, which thus achieved national recognition. In the midst of the antifascist war, Congress invited people to recite the Pledge with their right hand on their heart—to discourage the habit of doing so with the arm raised and rigid, with palms facing upward, a greeting that had a long history but that now, suddenly, seemed too similar to the Nazi salute. Nor was the reciting of the Pledge made compulsory by this or any other federal act. It is the state laws that deal with this matter, and to this day it is encouraged in only half the states.

In 1954, in the midst of the Cold War and the anticommunist struggle, Congress again changed the Pledge of Allegiance and named God in it. The final and present version, therefore, sounds like this: "I pledge allegiance to the flag of the United States of America and to the Republic for which it stands, one Nation under God, indivisible, with liberty and justice for all." The added words echo Lincoln's Gettysburg Address, which I have already mentioned, in particular the famous conclusion in which Lincoln says that "this nation, under God, shall have a new birth of freedom—and that government of the people, by the people, for the people, shall not perish from the earth." During and after the war, the "under God" phrase had become quite familiar, uttered in various presidential speeches by Franklin Roosevelt, Harry Truman, and Dwight Eisenhower. The pressure for formal change in the Pledge came from the usual suspects, the patriotic associations; the initiative in this case was from the Knights of Columbus, a Catholic fraternal organization. The intentions of the legislators, in their bipartisan efforts, were explicit. At this moment in our history, they affirmed, the principles that inspire the American government and the American way of life "are under attack by a system whose philosophy is at direct odds with our own." The American system, they said, paraphrasing the Declaration of Independence, is founded on the principle that each individual is important because he has been created by God and has been endowed with certain unalienable rights that no one can usurp. Hence, a House of Representatives report came to this conclusion:

> The inclusion of God in our pledge therefore would further acknowledge the dependence of our people and our Government upon the moral directions of the Creator. At the same time it would serve to deny the atheistic and materialistic concepts of communism with its attendant subservience of the individual.[10]

President Eisenhower signed the law on June 14, 1954, Flag Day, and declared in a brief statement, "From this day forward, the millions of our school children will daily proclaim . . . the dedication of our Nation and our people to the Almighty." Eisenhower was convinced that a belief in the Almighty was necessary for the well-being of the republic, even if he was rather indifferent from a doctrinal point of view. As he once put it, "Our government makes no sense unless it is founded in a deeply felt religious faith—and I do not care what it is."[11] In the same spirit, in those years the federal government included God everywhere. In 1952, Congress established an annual National Day of Prayer, which, since 1988, is held the first Thursday of May; it also assigned a specific room in the Capitol as a place of prayer for congressmen. The White House inaugurated a presidential National Prayer Breakfast. In 1955, it was again Congress that added the words "In God We Trust" to banknotes, extending to them a feature that until then, beginning in 1864, was only compulsory for coins. (In the early twentieth century, President Theodore Roosevelt criticized this requirement because he felt it irreverent, almost sacrilegious, to involve God in questions of money.)[12] In 1956, Congress adopted "In God We Trust" as an official national motto, definitively putting aside the venerable, but never official, "E Pluribus Unum." Finally, it conferred the Congressional Gold Medal, the highest civilian award it can bestow, on the musician Irving Berlin for having composed, decades earlier, the song "God Bless America"—a sort of informal national anthem, much easier to remember and more pleasant to sing than "The Star-Spangled Banner."

II Freedom *Whose Freedom?*

4 God and the Flag

As discussed in the preceding chapter, the rituals surrounding the Stars and Stripes are quite recent. The shaping of their features, so highly infused with civil religiosity, has elicited many a conflict that has involved the citizens' civic and religious beliefs, the role of religion in public life, and the country's most sacred institutions. The school ceremonies of saluting the flag and reciting the Pledge of Allegiance have been one of the main causes of these conflicts, which started even before the Pledge made explicit reference to the Creator. The hostilities were begun in the 1930s by the Jehovah's Witnesses, a millenarian church that refuses any act of loyalty to secular governments, only recognizes the Kingdom of Christ, and interprets the precepts of the Bible literally. A Pennsylvania family of Witnesses refused to allow their children to take part in those ceremonies, then compulsory in the state schools, because they contradicted the biblical prohibition of worshipping images (Exodus 20:4–5). The children were expelled, and the episode gave rise to a court case centered on the Bill of Rights of the Constitution, in particular on the First Amendment, which prohibits the government from establishing an official religion and guarantees the right of individuals to the free exercise of their beliefs. The case reached the federal Supreme Court. And it seems only appropriate that to decide on these matters were called these nine august justices, eloquent and magniloquent, cryptic in their legal technicalities but with sudden flashes of hard-boiled common sense. They consider themselves the high priests of the political faith, the guardians of the temple in which are kept the sacred texts of the community's founding pact, the interpreters of the Word. And they are considered, said the Englishman James Bryce at the end of the nineteenth century, with a metaphor that today would be embarrassing, "a sort of Mecca, towards which the faces of the faithful [of the sacred science, law] turned."[1]

The justices, with a majority of eight to one, said that the Jehovah's Witnesses were in the wrong. In the decision *Minersville School District v. Gobitis* (1940), they maintained that states have the authority to provide for schoolchildren's civic education using whatever means they deem most appropriate and that these means cannot be called into question even by the Court itself. The oath and the salute to the flag come within this jurisdiction and do not violate any constitutional rights. Religious beliefs cannot exempt an individual from obeying a general law that does not aim at promoting or hindering a faith but rather aims at inspiring feelings of national cohesion. "The flag is the symbol of our national unity, transcending all internal differences," stated the Court, and "national unity is the basis of national security."[2] The justices, in effect, were saying that civic obligations are superior to religious ones and that the common civil cult of the flag is superior to the various religious cults present in society. The call to unity and national security was quite strong in 1940, when the Second World War was already under way and the United States was rearming. To many Americans it seemed that patriotism should take precedence over everything and against everyone. Against the Jehovah's Witnesses, who refused to compromise, there were acts of state repression and hostility on the part of public opinion, especially after the country actually entered the war. Other pupils were expelled; some were subjected to physical threats. The situation was becoming dangerous. The Court agreed to discuss a second similar case, and this time, in its decision in *West Virginia Board of Education v. Barnette* (1943), it overturned its previous ruling.

A few things had changed in the Supreme Court. There were two new justices, who had just been appointed by President Franklin D. Roosevelt; and Justice Harlan Fiske Stone, the only one who had been opposed to the majority decision in the *Gobitis* case, had become chief justice. Other things had changed in society; the antifascist war had increased sensitivity to forms of intolerance and ideological discipline that were typical of the enemy regimes. Precisely recalling the tragic experiences of "our present totalitarian enemies," the Court maintained that the First

Amendment, always and under any circumstances, protects individuals' freedom of conscience, even against the states' civic education programs, even in times of national emergency and heightened patriotism.[3] The ruling, written by Justice Robert H. Jackson (one of the recently appointed justices, who was subsequently the prosecuting attorney in the Nuremberg trials against the Nazi war criminals), contains resounding statements that today still find an echo in the public debate:

> Those who begin coercive elimination of dissent soon find themselves exterminating dissenters. Compulsory unification of opinion achieves only the unanimity of the graveyard.

And,

> There is no mysticism in the American concept of the State or of the nature or origin of its authority. We set up government by consent of the governed, and the Bill of Rights denies those in power any legal opportunity to coerce that consent. Authority here is to be controlled by public opinion, not public opinion by authority.
>
> If there is any fixed star in our constitutional constellation, it is that no official, high or petty, can prescribe what shall be orthodox in politics, nationalism, religion, or other matters of opinion or force citizens to confess by word or act their faith therein.

The Court concluded, with a majority of six to three, that the Pledge of Allegiance and the flag salute are a coercion and, if compulsory, are unconstitutional. In explaining the decision, Justice Jackson proposed some considerations that were in many ways surprising. There is no doubt, he said, that the salute to the flag is an expression of thought and that the flag is an important symbol, loved and revered. But symbols are by their very nature ambiguous and lend themselves to conflicting interpretations. "A person gets from a symbol the meaning he puts into it, and what is one man's comfort and inspiration is another's jest and scorn." Furthermore, the language of the Pledge of Allegiance is anything but neutral. The use of the term "Republic" instead of "democracy," or "one Nation" instead of "federation," calls up bitter disputes in the country's history and political culture. And the expression "freedom and justice for all," wrote Jackson with a very cool understatement, "if it must be accepted as descriptive of the present order rather than an ideal, might to some seem an overstatement." It is a question of differences of opinion. The purpose of the Bill of Rights is precisely to ensure that differences are expressed freely and without fear of intimidation by any majority, parliamentary or popular. There is no voting on this right; it does not depend on the outcome of an election. And it is not just about matters of little account—it would be too easy. "The test of its substance is the right to differ as to things that touch the heart of the existing order," crucial and sensitive issues such as, indeed, the national flag and what it represents.

Justice Felix Frankfurter, who was the author of the *Gobitis* decision, did not change his mind and wrote an impassioned dissenting opinion that more forcefully reaffirmed the arguments of three years earlier. He repeated that the Court should not interfere with the will of legislators who represent the people; that it is prohibited by the Constitution, by the principles of the separation of powers and federalism, by the principles of democracy; that judges are not a superlegislature: they must limit their activism, exercise judicial self-restraint. Above all, he repeated that what was at stake in the issue was not the right to freedom of religion but the very essence of the secular nature of government. Accepting that religious dogmas allow individuals or groups to disobey the law means accepting not the separation between state and church but, rather, the subordination of the former to the latter, "the subordination of the general civil authority of the state to sectarian scruples." It means recognizing not the equality of all but the privileges of some, their civil immunity; and that happens only in a theocracy. If it were to happen in the United States, a country where there are at least 250 different religious denominations, each one with different dogmas and scruples, it would simply be chaos. What would happen, Frankfurter asked himself, to compulsory conscription, obligatory vaccination or medical treatment, or the rules of food hygiene in the face of conscientious objections? And why exclude that there might be objections to "the poisoning of impressionable minds of children by chauvinistic teaching of history"? These are not fantasies, he recalled with mordant irony, since many people believe that "nationalism is the seed-bed of war."

With the *Barnette* decision, the rites of the school cult of the flag became voluntary, and that is how they are today. Even in states that provide for them by law, there is no obligation to participate either for teachers or for students. Nevertheless, the controversies have not died down and have focused on the words of the Pledge of Allegiance added in 1954, those that place the nation "under God" and multiply the religious implications of the oath. For decades, secularist groups and atheists have fought to have those words deleted, seeing them as a sectarian fundamentalist attempt to appropriate the Stars and Stripes and give it a confessional meaning, and therefore, once again, as a violation of the Bill of Rights. The conservative religious groups have instead defended them, and some have gone further. They have launched campaigns to superimpose on the flag the motto "One Nation under God," although the Flag Code prohibits the superimposition of anything on the flag, or to change the end of the oath to "with freedom and justice for all, born and unborn," in order to express their condemnation of abortion. In the 1970s, moreover, several radical groups sought to introduce the language of multiculturalism in the Pledge, proposing to talk about "one Nation of many people, cultures, languages, and colors under God, indivisible, with respect, liberty, and justice for all."[4] The proposal was unsuccessful. And it had a singular characteristic: it made the oath multicultural and pluralistic but was careful to avoid bringing into question its appeal to the deity. The question, in short, has become political dynamite, and legislators have preferred to give it a wide berth and leave it, once again, to the federal judges—appointed for life, protected by the Constitution, not subject to electoral tests.

And so in 2002 the presence of God in the Pledge of Allegiance finally came before a high court—not the Supreme Court but just one step below it, namely, the Federal Court of Appeals based in San Francisco, California. A section of that court said that secularists and atheists were right. The clause *under God*, says the decision in *Newdow v. U.S. Congress*, constitutes a profession of faith, faith in monotheism. It communicates to students, even those who choose not to repeat the Pledge, that the institutions believe in the existence of a supreme being and therefore that people who do not believe are foreign to the community. This appears to be the imposition of a religious orthodoxy. The First Amendment, says the decision, prohibits the government from supporting not only a particular religion at the expense of another but also religion at the expense of atheism; it also protects the rights of nonbelievers. The clause *under God* is therefore unconstitutional, as is the law that introduced it.[5] The judgment could not have occurred at a more delicate moment. Made public in June 2002, it offered an ironic counterpoint to the official patriotic rhetoric following September 11, 2001, and the war in Afghanistan. And the decision was overwhelmed by that rhetoric. The politicians' and commentators' insults rained down on it with bipartisan vehemence. "Ridiculous," it was called by President George W. Bush, and in contrast with the sentiments of the country: "America is a nation that values our relationship with an Almighty." "Wrong," Congress almost unanimously categorized it in a resolution that, moreover, confirmed "that God remains in our motto." Members of the House of Representatives, many with Stars-and-Stripes ties, repeated the Pledge, en masse, on the Capitol steps, as excited as if they had gone back to school.[6]

In fact, the judge who had issued the decision (accused of being a "liberal extremist" even though he was a Republican appointed by President Richard Nixon) had suspended its enforcement, pending a reconsideration by the court in convened sessions. The new and more authoritative decision, made in February 2003, confirmed the previous one, albeit in an attenuated form; in fact, it limited its application to the state of California, where the case had arisen, without touching the federal act of 1954. One of the judges remembered that the courts cannot and must not bow to public or political pressures, the more so when dealing with constitutional principles, the more so in times of national crisis, because "it is then that our freedoms and our liberties are in the greatest peril."[7] It was anything but a routine statement in the once again patriotically inflamed climate of the days preceding the war with Iraq, a climate that made the Supreme Court very cautious when the case finally came to its attention—so cautious that, with an anticlimactic decision and a clever political move, in June 2004 it reversed the Court of Appeals' ruling, but on a technicality.[8] The justices dodged the thorny questions that they should have discussed, if they had wanted to go to the core of the matter: the broader questions of God being referred to so often in the nation's public rituals, in the Pledge but also in the national anthem and the national motto, and in so many oaths (the swearing in of presidents, of new naturalized citizens, of witnesses in trials). Is it just a way of solemnizing public occasions, a form of ceremonial deism, as many people say, which has lost any confessional meaning, even any meaning *tout court*? Or is it something more significant? Among other things, the sessions of the Supreme Court itself open with the invocation "God Save the United States and This Honorable Court!"

5 The Land of the Free

That the flag was associated with the idea of conflict and freedom, a freedom of revolutionary origin, was obvious from the outset. As I have already mentioned, in the prints of the early republican period the Stars and Stripes goes hand in hand with the keywords of the American Revolution, the images of the liberty tree or the liberty goddess and that symbol of international Euro-Atlantic subversion, the Phrygian cap.[1] And the same association is evident in the first patriotic songs, with European influences of a different type, some of them rather ironic. In "America" (1831), the banner of the "sweet land of liberty" is saluted, even if, through an unforgivable distraction of the author, the greeting is sung on the notes of "God Save the King," the anthem of hated England. In "The Star-Spangled Banner" (1814), the most famous theme is that of the starred cloth that waves "o'er the land of the free and the home of the brave." The poem is by Francis Scott Key, a lawyer and amateur minstrel who, having witnessed the British bombardment of Fort McHenry in Baltimore during the Anglo-American war of 1812, was inspired by the sight of the flag, which, although reduced to shreds, was still fluttering on the fort after the battle. His composition was set to music and grew in popularity during the nineteenth century. Also in this case, the borrowed melody is English, though of less formal and less respectable origins; it belongs to a drinking song, very well known at the time on both sides of the Atlantic. Despite some misgivings (a drunkards' song?), this origin did not prevent "The Star-Spangled Banner" from finally being elevated to the honored rank of national anthem of the United States. Furthermore, it is from the song's text that is derived the motto "In God We Trust"—from the verse that says,

> Then conquer we must, when our cause it is just,
> And this be our motto: "In God is our trust."[2]

The Civil War strengthened the link between the star-spangled banner and freedom, at least in the Unionist North and particularly among African Americans, be they free or slave. In the antislavery war, that link seemed purer, finally free of ambiguity and stains. The flag of the Revolution and the Spirit of '76 became the flag of the Spirit of the North,[3] a spirit that hovers in the songs that followed the Northern troops to the battlefields, including brand-new songs such as "The Stars and Stripes" and "The Battle Cry of Freedom":

> Yes, we'll rally 'round the flag, boys
> We'll rally once again
> Shouting the battle cry
> Of freedom.[4]

Speakers and editors sang the praises of "the symbol of Equal Rights, of Law, of Country, and, above all, Universal Liberty," which has ceased to cover the oppression of slavery ("Thank God! Its stains are washed away") and is therefore even more loved—a symbol for which, they repeated, it is an honor to shed one's blood and it is sweet and glorious to die.[5] When Lincoln spoke at a solemn flag-raising ceremony at Independence Hall in Philadelphia, the birthplace of the Declaration of Independence, the newspapers commented that the beauty of the Stars and Stripes had never been so fully recognized and loyalty to the land of the free, over which it flutters, so publicly declared. The abolitionists extolled the free men who defended the flag against "The Spirit of the South." And black abolitionists called on "every colored man able to bear arms to rally around the flag," to destroy racially based slavery and attempt, once the war was over, in the defeated and militarily occupied South, a bold experiment of multiracial democracy in the years of Reconstruction.[6]

However, even in the postwar period, it was not at all clear who really had the right to citizenship in the land of the free. After all, even the Southern rebels had appealed to continuity with the Spirit of '76 to proclaim the legitimacy of states' rights and Southern independence, to defend *their* freedom as whites and their peculiar institution, black slavery. Although forced by circumstances to change flag, they had immediately invented one that, intentionally, was very similar to the flag just cast aside. One of their battle songs, entitled, with arrogant defiance, "The Flag of Secession," was in effect a shameless plagiarism of "The Star-Spangled Banner"; it preserved the theme music and changed the words to fit the new purpose:

> Oh, such is the welcome the Southron bestows
> On the minions who strive to make slaves of a nation,
> We've a hand for our friends but the sword for our foes.
> . . . .
> And the Northmen shall shrink from our warriors' might,
> And the flag of secession in triumph shall wave
> O'er the land of the freed and the home of the brave.[7]

In other words, the slave South was anything but alien to the revolutionary and patriotic tradition and the rhetoric of freedom; and when the war was over and slavery abolished, it used that tradition and rhetoric to try to "put the blacks back in their place," establish racial segregation, reaffirm white supremacy and white freedom. And before, during, and after the war, even in the North, important sections of white public opinion waved patriotism and the Stars and Stripes to limit the civil liberties of the citizens of African origin.[8]

The fact is that, historically, the revolutionary tradition of freedom was a complicated, racialized affair. The American Revolution, in its founding documents, had proclaimed great ideals in a universalistic language that, however, for many, applied only to the universe of whites. The fathers of the republic took for granted that enslaved Africans, like the native inhabitants of the continent, were not members of the political community. Even those among them who abhorred slavery refused to accept blacks as citizens; they considered them foreign to the discourse, announced with radical tones in the Declaration of Independence, of equality ("all men are created equal") and freedom (an "unalienable" right, also warranted by the Supreme Creator). It is no coincidence that the Declaration is silent on slavery—and it is a deafening silence that reveals the existence of a secret civic oath among its signatories, an oath of exclusion. And the Constitution skirts the issue or is also silent. To be more precise, it recognizes and incorporates the institution of slavery in the machine of the new federal government, encouraging its consolidation in the Southern states where it was already prevalent, it but does so with hypocritical and ambiguous words. In order not to sully the sacred text, not to mention the unmentionable, it refers to slaves as no better specified "other persons," clearly distinct from "free persons" who form the sovereign people, the "We, the People" that is the source and foundation of everything. The word "slavery" appears for the first time in the Constitution only when slavery was abolished throughout the country—with the Thirteenth Amendment of 1865.[9]

But this is only a part of the story. There is also another part, equally and perhaps even more important. Once enunciated, the language of freedom (and equality) had acquired an autonomous force, an authority that went beyond the original and true intentions of its first codifiers. The first abolitionists, already active at the time of the Revolution, took that language seriously, gave it a universal value, and appropriated it to ask for freedom for everyone, without racial distinctions; it was also thanks to this impetus that slavery gradually disappeared in the Northern states, although racial equality remained a mirage. A great African American abolitionist of the next generation, Frederick Douglass, bore witness to this political and intellectual appropriation in an impassioned speech for the Fourth of July 1852. Douglass, who was born a slave, addressed white Americans, accusing them of being inconsistent with their history because they tolerated the servitude of their black brothers. He reminded them of "the great principles of political freedom and of natural justice" of the Declaration of Independence to say that they were being betrayed every day: "This Fourth of July is yours, not mine"; "I am not included within the pale of this glorious anniversary!" But he also said that in those principles resided his and his people's hope of redemption and liberation. With a surprising act of historical revisionism, in order to nail whites to their sense of guilt for the present, Douglass even extolled the Constitution as "a glorious liberty document," refusing to admit, against all the evidence, that it condoned slavery.[10]

Radical white abolitionists such as William Lloyd Garrison were more drastic. They used the language of freedom not to praise or to interpret the Constitution to their own advantage but to attack it, to denounce it as a proslavery pact ("a covenant with death," "an agreement with hell") and to burn it in the streets—and even to insult the flag. In their propaganda posters, the Stars and Stripes is depicted as it shamelessly flutters on the shameful slave markets of the South or on the courts of the whole country engaged in hunting fugitive slaves; the flagpole is transformed into a whipping tree to which black men are tied hands and feet. In their speeches, the national colors acquire a sinister meaning: the red stripes are the blood shed by the slaves. In their newspapers, they repeat the verses of the British poet Thomas Campbell:

> United States, your banner wears
> Two emblems—one of hunger;
> Alas, the other that it bears,
> Reminds us of your shame.
> The white man's liberty entype
> Stands blazoned by your stars;
> But what's the meaning of the stripes?
> They mean your Negro-scars.[11]

It was only with the Civil War that the flag truly changed into a symbol of liberation and that its red color became a symbol of the blood not of black victims but, rather, of black heroes, those heroes who had sacrificed their lives on the altar of freedom. Following the victory of the North, Douglass claimed for himself "the national flag, which I could now call mine, in common with other American citizens." He knew he had brought to fruition a great battle for freedom. He also knew that he immediately had to start another, against segregation and racism.[12]

The American Revolution, in short, had not produced a clear-cut, definitive set of principles and practices of freedom, ready for use on any occasion. On the contrary, from the Revolution there had emerged a multiplicity of ideal and social traditions, different and conflicting, experimental and unfinished, contaminated and dirty, in which the freedom of some could mean the nonfreedom of others. And every tradition boasted of having the Stars and Stripes on its side. This is true for every revolution or social transformation; the perfect and universal regenerative event, which frees everyone forever, exists only in the imagination of revolutionaries, at least of those who are the winners in any given moment, and in the posthumous and retrospective rhetoric of patriots. From this point of view one can say that the Revolution had never finished; it continued to stir society well after its official conclusion (wasn't the Civil War the second American Revolution?). This also created a strong sense of uncertainty, because freedom, the specific idea that each person or social group had of it, seemed something never definitively acquired, always threatened, fragile and delicate, to be defended with a constant vigilance that could perhaps lead to a touch of paranoia.[13] In fact, in the text of "The Star-Spangled Banner," that the flag still flutters on the land of the free is said, at the end of the first verse, in a doubting and interrogative form; only in the final verse does it say that this is the way it is and will be in the future. And those interrogative lines

> Oh, say does that star-spangled banner yet wave
> O'er the land of the free and the home of the brave?

are often cited by people who want to raise controversial questions about the state of freedom in the country, and to complain about it.

6 Multiple Traditions

The multiplicity of traditions symbolized by the national flag concerns not only the race question in a particular historical period but all the political and social issues in the country throughout its history. For immigrants, the flag of the United States was and is the emblem of freedom, promised and found, of citizenship and a decent life, but also of forced Americanization and nativist and xenophobic rejection. In recognition of freedom and citizenship, immigrants and hyphenated Americans of an older immigration, on some occasions, display the Stars and Stripes side by side with the flag of their countries of origin. Thus they proclaim their common patriotism and at the same time their own specific historical roots, their consensual attachment to the New World and their distinct descents from Old Worlds.[1] For over a century, for example, Italian Americans have been celebrating Columbus Day and their identity with the American ("my country") and Italian colors (the tricolor, "my heritage"). But what today is taken for granted was not at all so at the end of the nineteenth century, when the commemoration of the Catholic and Latin Christopher Columbus, or of other non-Anglo-Saxon and non-Protestant heroes, was a challenge to the nativist flags that, from time to time, had fluttered at least since the anti-Irish, anti-Catholic, and antipapist crusades of the 1840s. The challenge was won when Columbus became everyone's hero, with the quadricentennial celebrations of 1892. That year, Columbus Day became an official holiday, thanks, among other things, to the pressure from the promoters of the Pledge of Allegiance. For the Irish Catholics, the Italians, and later the Hispanics, it was and is a way of demonstrating their Americanness; for the authorities, it was a way of Americanizing them.

A photograph of 1919 shows how the relationship between immigrants and the flag is still more complex. It is a photograph of the historical

Liberty Golda Meir as Liberty in Poale Chasidim Pageant, Milwaukee, Wisconsin, May 18, 1919. Photograph by Albert Kuhli. (Golda Meir Collection, Archives Department, University of Wisconsin–Milwaukee Libraries)

pageant acted out by a group of immigrants in Milwaukee, Wisconsin, with the sponsorship of the Americanization Society. Under a star-spangled banner, a man plays the part of Abraham Lincoln, and a woman plays the Statue of Liberty, with the inscription "The Wanderer finds Liberty in America." The actors are Jewish Zionist immigrants, and the woman is Goldie Meyerson, who was to become Golda Meir and was to find her freedom elsewhere, in the state of Israel, under another flag. In the eyes of young Golda, the United States was probably only a place of transition, a stage toward another project of liberation (certainly similar to the American one, also based on a promised land); and her bowing to the Stars and Stripes was a temporary act. But for many Jewish immigrants, it was, instead, a definitive act.

It was a Jewish British writer, Israel Zangwill, who popularized the phrase "melting pot," which he used as the title for a successful theatrical production. The play, *The Melting Pot* (1908), which opens under the sign of a Stars and Stripes that decorates the interior of a New York apartment, tells of the troubled love story between a Jewish boy and a Russian girl whose parents were anti-Semites in the Old World. Can they continue to be anti-Semites in the New World? Of course not. After many trials and tribulations, European prejudices are overcome, there is a reconciliation, and love triumphs. The end of the play has a prophetic tone. The contented lovers say: "There she lies, the great Melting Pot. . . . Ah, what a stirring and a seething! Celt and Latin, Slav and Teuton, Greek and Syrian,—black and yellow," and of course "Jew and Gentile." There is room for everyone, and from their amorous union something new is born.[2]

Zangwill's vision was too simple and optimistic. As in other moments of the country's history, during and after the First World War, Stars-and-Stripes patriotism again acquired an intolerant character of xenophobic exclusion. And it presented its harder, more extreme and extremist face. The pamphlet *The Religion of Old Glory* (1918) by William Norman Guthrie proposed, with fervid prose, creating a national cult of the flag that would make it an object of veneration for the masses and a symbol of the organic link between the leader and the nation, or rather the white nation, in fact, the *folk*. The nation had the right to impose observance of this worship and to exclude from the community the different and disobedient. In August 1925, the capital of the United States witnessed a demonstration by the organization that most violently expressed these sentiments, namely, the Invisible Empire, the Knights of the Ku Klux Klan. The KKK only recruited white Protestant males and was hostile to blacks and immigrants, Jews and Catholics, liberals, trade unionists, and suffragists; it believed that all these people were a threat to the most genuine national values, white male supremacy and "100% Americanism," which were the true legacy of the American Revolution. The Klansmen were fanatical about the flag, claiming its ideal ownership; they asked new members to swear on it, and they reproduced it everywhere, together

Parades September 13, 1926: members of the American white-supremacist movement, the Ku Klux Klan, marching down Pennsylvania Avenue in Washington, D.C. (Prints and Photographs Division, Library of Congress)

Parades March 3, 1913: head of woman-suffrage parade, Washington, D.C. (Prints and Photographs Division, Library of Congress)

with two other objects sacred to them, the Bible and the cross (often in flames). Forty thousand of them marched in Washington, along Pennsylvania Avenue, with the Capitol in the background, in a forest of Stars and Stripes.[3]

In the 1920s, the intolerant religion of Old Glory crossed its path with forms of Protestant religious revival that took the name of "fundamentalism." The term derives from a series of pamphlets entitled *The Fundamentals* (1909), which claimed that the Bible, interpreted literally, contains the guiding principles essential for the Christian life in all its aspects. These ideas were already present in the religious revivalism of the previous century; now they reemerged to counter modern society, culture, and science. The pamphlets sold millions of copies, mainly in the South and West of the country. The organizations that drew inspiration from them attacked the Darwinian theories on the origin and evolution of species as blasphemous and contrary to the biblical account of divine creation; and they fought for patriotic causes that were in tune with those of the nativists and the KKK. A radical exponent of this union was the former fundamentalist preacher and former Klansman Gerald L. K. Smith. A political agitator and clever radio speaker in the 1930s, Smith founded a small Christian Nationalist Party, in 1942, which advocated defending the white nation against the hybridization of races, the Christian nation against the Jewish conspiracy, the American system against communism and fascism, and finally, the independence of the United States against international alliances and organizations such as the United Nations. Its monthly magazine, with an admirable synthesis of different but converging ideological pulsions, which had already become intertwined in the rituals and sinister iconography of the KKK, was called *The Cross and the Flag*.[4]

The most famous photograph of the 1925 KKK rally surprisingly recalls another one, taken twelve years earlier: exactly the same view, the same perspective, the same stretch of Pennsylvania Avenue, the same background with the Capitol, the same Stars and Stripes. But this time those who are marching in Washington, in 1913, are women suffragists.

The similarity between the two demonstrations could not be clearer, nor could there be a more dramatic contrast in the respective appeals to the values of the flag—the limitation of citizenship in the first case, its enlargement to new subjects in the second case. The struggle of the suffragists had, from its very first pronouncements, aimed at being an extension of the principles of the Spirit of '76 beyond the boundaries of gender within which they were conceived. The "Seneca Falls Declaration of Sentiments and Resolutions" of 1848 was, in fact, a polemical and effective rewriting of the Declaration of Independence in a gender-egalitarian key, starting from one of its most famous statements: the change to "all men and women are created equal." The resulting request for civil equality and the political franchise clashed with the beliefs of the Founding Fathers, who had in mind a male and patriarchal republic but could be understood in the context of the revolutionary discourse on individual rights.[5] Similar appeals for rights have been made by homosexual movements, using the same rituals. The 1979 Gay and Lesbian March in Washington offers photographic images that reflect those of 1913 and 1925: once again the Capitol, Pennsylvania Avenue (now without the streetcar lines), the flags (now finally in bright color pictures).

I have not found images of Washington marches by the labor movement, but elsewhere and in other circumstances the ritual of the Stars and Stripes has also been repeated in its rallies and struggles: a protest procession in Denver led by Mother Jones in 1903; Lawrence textile workers with flags confronting Massachusetts militiamen with fixed bayonets in 1912; a South Appalachian woman striker, in 1929, taking her stand in court with red, white, and blue dress and cap ("I was born under it, guess I have a right to [dress in it]");[6] miners and electrical workers taking to the streets in the 1930s and 1940s; California farmworkers following César Chávez in the 1960s and 1970s. Workers on strike have often displayed the national colors to proclaim the patriotism of their claims and their rights, with a language that has its roots in the popular republicanism that is one of the ingredients and legacies of the American Revolution. The message is clear: the rights the employers want to deny and trample on are "American rights" of freedom and fairness; it is the employers who are being unpatriotic and un-American, even though they themselves try to hide behind the colors of the flag; "unionism is the spirit of Americanism." In fact, for several generations after 1776, the Fourth of July was celebrated by workers and trade unions as a sort of labor festival. It is from there that originates the Labor Day that in the United States is celebrated on the first Monday in September with a large deployment of national flags. The Stars-and-Stripes Labor Day seems, and often has been, in ideological competition with the international May Day of the socialist red flag; and yet it came first and not in opposition with May Day. It arose in 1882, anticipating the events (in any case equally American) of 1886, which gave rise to the First of May festivities, and it was the victory of a strong autochthonous working-class movement. It came into being on a Monday in tribute to the Anglo-American tradition of Saint Monday, the day of nonworking and great drinking that the craftsmen took to make up for Sunday's pious labors. All this was and is an expression of a working-class Americanism that has marked the history of the United States in the nineteenth and twentieth centuries, making it, to some extent, different from the history of the rest of the industrialized West.[7]

In many cases, the use of the national flag also has the aim of offering symbolic protection against the attacks of opponents or of explicitly provoking a clash over who really possesses its truest meaning. In the early 1960s, Martin Luther King, Jr.'s civil rights movement organized nonviolent marches in the segregated South precisely where it knew that the local authorities were more short-tempered, nervous, and racist, expecting a scandalously violent response, in fact wanting it; it was a way, said King, to "dramatize the existence of injustice." In Birmingham and Selma, Alabama, sheriffs Eugene "Bull" Connor and Jim Clark did not know how to control their instincts and unleashed the police against the marchers. The newspapers and television stations circulated, throughout the country, images of black men, women, and children being attacked with water cannons, tear gas, sticks, whips, and police dogs. Also under attack was the Stars and Stripes, in which the demonstrators were

Liberty Crowd of strikers with flags menacing strike-breakers, confronted by soldiers, Lawrence, Massachusetts (c. 1912). (Prints and Photographs Division, Library of Congress)

wrapped, shown in so many famous photographs from the final phase of the march from Selma to Montgomery in 1965. In addition, the local racist counterdemonstrators marched with the old Southern battle colors, the Southern Cross (and sometimes with the most ribald flags of the American Revolution, those with the rattlesnake and the inscription "Don't Tread on Me"); Sheriff Connor invited people to "raise the Confederate flag as did our forefathers and tell [the Negroes], 'You shall not pass.'" It seemed that the Civil War was not really over and that, once again, it was the federal government in Washington that was being challenged. Partly as a consequence of these sensational events, Congress passed the Civil Rights Act of 1964 and the Voting Rights Act of 1965.[8]

Civil rights Participants, some carrying American flags, marching in the civil rights march from Selma to Montgomery, Alabama, in 1965. Photograph by Peter Pettus. (Prints and Photographs Division, Library of Congress)

Civil rights and busing "Soiling of Old Glory," Boston 1976. (Copyright Stanley Forman, 1976)

Ten years later, an episode of a contrasting indication signaled that the wind was changing and that the battle over rights and the flag had moved north. Attempts at racial integration in Boston's public school system, de facto segregated because of the inhabitants' residential segregation, provoked strong negative reactions in the white working-class neighborhoods. The Irish Americans of South Boston, in particular, violently opposed busing—the practice of transferring by bus black children to schools in white neighborhoods and white children to schools in black districts. They organized protest demonstrations, waving flags, singing patriotic songs, repeating the Pledge of Allegiance, assaulting colored citizens. In this heated climate, on April 5, 1976, during a rally in front of city hall, a white student, using a flagstaff like a spear, assaulted Theodore Landsmark, a black lawyer who was passing by. The student struck Landsmark right in the face, while comrades shouting "Get the nigger" punched and kicked him.[9] The photograph of the incident has become a well-known, and notorious, icon, for its incisive and symbolic significance. The Stars and Stripes is here literally being brandished as an instrument of war to defend the purity of a contested civic space, to keep out those who are perceived as dangerous strangers. It is easy to imagine that, in the eyes of the more radical African Americans, this would prove that the national banner was, in effect, a weapon against them (someone tried "to kill me with the American flag," commented Landsmark). The opinion of the press photographer who took the picture, Stanley Forman of the *Boston Herald American*, is more nuanced and problematic. In fact, he called the photograph, which won the Pulitzer Prize, "The Soiling of Old Glory."

7 American Jeremiad

The disputes about the flag have a solid basis. The patriotic tradition of the United States is not only a celebration of America as it is; it also contains elements for a noncelebratory vision, for a critique of the status quo and plans for change, to imagine America as it should be. And words count: when one makes the lexical leap from the *United States* to *America*, one is leaping from the prose of history to the poetry of myth. In the mythical-prophetic language on which this tradition is based, it says that America is the destination of a journey of liberation, a promised land. The paradigm is that of the biblical Exodus; interpreted in a religious key by some of the early immigrants (the Puritans of New England), later becoming the secular heritage of all the British North American colonies and, after 1776, of the revolutionary political community, it renews itself with each immigrant wave. But just as the book of Exodus says, the promised land is not easy to reach; it is, in fact, a promise, not a certainty to be taken for granted. And the journey carries the risk of embarking on wrong paths and dead ends; it involves dangers and the risk of failure. Like the Jews fleeing from slavery in Egypt toward the land of Canaan, the Americans fleeing from the inferno of the Old World will also stray from the designated path, will pursue false values and build bad institutions, re-creating a hell in the Eden of the New World, and will be punished. They may, however, redeem themselves by denouncing, fighting, and defeating the enemy who has installed himself among them and by regaining the original values and formulating a new prophecy. The tension between the perfection of the promise and the imperfection of life, between ideals and reality, is therefore part of the national ideology; it is the essence of a ritual lamentation that has been defined as the "American jeremiad."[1]

The logic of the jeremiad has conferred legitimacy on social and political conflict. It has provided arguments for individuals and groups of every persuasion, each determined to redeem America from its guilty deviations, lead it back to the right path, and give its own version of this right path. Each has resolved to achieve its ideal America, sometimes accusing opponents of being anti-American or, rather, which is even worse, un-American—that is, alien to America, aliens who have come from other worlds, perhaps conspirators in league with evil. Calls to arms of this kind are everywhere, and not only in the most eccentric, radical, or reactionary movements of which I have spoken in the preceding chapters. They are, in effect, part of everyday politics and party politics. Twentieth-century liberals, mainly Democrats, have raised the scandal of the discrepancy between the original American promise and social marginalization, racial discrimination, inequality, and poverty and have called for corrective action by the government. As in a Hollywood film condemned to a happy ending, their analysis and their solutions have sometimes lost dramatic force in the grand finale; after passionately describing a nightmare, they prescribe small acceptable recipes as a remedy—a reform, a law, and America will be saved. On the other hand, the late-twentieth-century conservatives, mainly Republicans, have accused the liberals of having betrayed the true nature of that promise, of having brought the country to ruin through a century of statist errors. And they have proposed starting again from pre-1900 truths with reasoning that, to remain in the realm of Hollywood cinema, recalls a successful title, *Back to the Future* (1985).

These phenomena are anything but unknown to other political or national traditions born of revolutionary events and ideas. Every revolution, with the benefit of hindsight, is the proclamation of many different worlds and many unrealized possibilities that can be recovered by returning to their uncontaminated source. In the name of these "recoveries," the heirs of that same revolution, and the same flag, can tear one another to pieces in fierce battles. This has happened where the revolution has become a shared heritage, the very foundation of national identity, and therefore a terrain open to different interpretations that aim at building distinct political identities within the nation. This dynamic applies to the American Revolution—and to the French Revolution as well.

"Mother of the political culture into which all of us are born," wrote historian François Furet, the French Revolution "allows everyone to look for filiations," and for two hundred years these searches have clashed. The famous slogan "*Liberté, Egalité, Fraternité*," permits, in effect, at least three revolutionary narratives: constitutional (the narrative of freedom), democratic and popular (the narrative of equality), and national or patriotic (the narrative of fraternity).[2] This multiplicity of narrations has also applied to revolutionary movements with more controversial and less established results, such as the socialist and communist ones. They too have cultivated their jeremiads in which the theme of deviation from the original purposes, and of betrayal, constantly resurfaces—to justify specific strategies claiming to be more authentic than others and, in any case, to confirm the perfection of the ideal despite the imperfections of history. And how many conflicts there have been about the true meaning and ownership of the Red flag! That all this history is reminiscent of the dynamics of some religious movements, particularly those fundamentalisms (Western and non-Western) that preach a return to the old faith as a response to the deceit they perceive in the society around them, is probably not a coincidence. It is probably not only the American ideology that has religious roots.

In the United States, even the Communists, despite being the offspring of another revolution, have proclaimed themselves to be the true heirs of the American Revolution and its promises. In the 1930s, in addressing the classic question "Who Are the Americans?" the party secretary, Earl Browder, had no doubts: "we are the Americans and Communism is the Americanism of the twentieth century." The revolutionary tradition, he wrote, was the soul of Americanism, and the Communists were the only ones who consciously perpetuated those traditions and applied them to present-day problems. At the time of the Popular Front, which saw their greatest successes and the hope of attaining respectability, the Communists created a political pedigree for themselves that enlisted in the cause, and in truly nonpartisan spirit, the great national heroes, the Federalist Washington, the Democratic Jefferson, the Republican Lincoln; Jefferson was hailed as the forefather of those Americans who fight "against the tyranny of Big Business with the revolutionary spirit and boldness with which he fought the Tories of that day." In fact, they went even further, extolling the personal genealogical tree of Browder, who boasted ancestors among the first settlers of Virginia and the fighters in the Revolution; in other words, they said, "the Browders have a right to say that they are among the founders of America." It was thus that the party greeted May Day, quite correctly indeed, as "Made in America!": "as American as the Fourth of July—And the Declaration of Independence." And then they celebrated an Americanism Week, sang "The Star-Spangled Banner" at their meetings, and often replaced the Red flag with the Stars and Stripes. All this, of course, did not save the Communists from government repression when hard times came, when they were singled out as the quintessence of un-Americanism.[3]

None better than Langston Hughes, African American poet and singer of the beauty of black culture ("I am a Negro—and beautiful!"),[4] a communist sympathizer, has expressed the dramatic tension inherent in the idea of America, tensions between the glittering promise and the opaque reality but also between opaque reality and the possibilities of the promise. In some of his most popular verses of the 1930s, he contrasted the American founding myth of liberty, opportunity, and equality with the brutal historical fact that "America never was America to me." But he also appealed to the equally historical fact that change and redemption are feasible and implied in the founding myth itself: "Let America be the dream the dreamers dreamed." Said Hughes,

> O, let America be America again—
> The land that never has been yet—
> And yet must be—the land where every man is free.

And,

> O, Yes,
> I say it plain,

America never was America to me,
And yet I swear this oath—
America will be![5]

It is no small paradox that this descendant of black abolitionists and heir to the culture of people who in America have been enslaved should have adopted such a seemingly nostalgic tone about the American past and indeed titled this poem of his, nostalgically, "Let America Be America Again" (1936). The paradox is not only his. It belongs to W. E. B. Du Bois ("Not America but what America might be—the Real America") as well as, of course, to Martin Luther King.[6] And it has never excluded rage and pessimism when racial oppression seemed as unyielding as a boulder. In the early 1950s, a more pessimistic Hughes wrote harder and more threatening words:

What happens to a dream deferred?
Does it dry up
Like a raisin in the sun?
. . . .
Or does it explode?[7]

In effect, it seems that only a few Americans have regarded themselves as being outside the discursive universe of the jeremiad, of the magic rhetorical circle of Americanism—pledging allegiance to other flags. And I do not mean here the Southerners who in the 1860s raised the Confederate ensigns of secession or who still fly them as symbols of regional or racial identity: they claimed then and still claim today to represent the most genuine spirit of America. I mean rather some other movements, born in particular social contexts. That the United States is a country of immigrants, protagonists of an exodus of liberation, is a reiterated definition that does not tell the whole truth. Not all its residents are immigrants or voluntary immigrants. Among them are the native peoples who have endured the exodus; like the original inhabitants of the biblical Canaan, they have been excluded from the alliance with the chosen people of the conquerors, subjugated and almost destroyed. There are the Mexicans annexed with the war of 1846–47; they did not come to the United States, but rather it was the United States that went to them. There are the Africans for whom the transatlantic voyage was a deportation in slavery and who have dreamed of a "counterexodus" of freedom to other promised lands, in Africa or elsewhere. Native Americans, Mexicans, and Africans have certainly fought for their American rights of citizenship under the Stars and Stripes. And yet their history has sanctioned the emergence of political and cultural groups that have spoken the language of alternative nationalisms, that have imagined their peoples as separate nations, and that have invented other flags with other colors: the red, black, and green (and sometimes gold) of black nationalism; the red with a white crescent and star of the first Nation of Islam; the red with a stylized black eagle of Mexican Americans; the various combinations of the different Native American nations. And it is understandable that a chief of the Stockbridge Mohican Indians, John Wannuaucon Quinney, could make a Fourth of July speech, in 1854, in some ways similar to the almost contemporary one of Frederick Douglass but, unlike that one, totally devoid of hope. For me, said Quinney, Independence Day is the feast of "a people, who occupy by conquest, or have usurped the possession of the territories of my fathers" and have brought "a train of terrible miseries, to end when my race shall have ceased to exist."[8]

Not all nationalists of this type have necessarily expressed a marked aversion to the Stars and Stripes. Not everyone has pronounced words of fire like Malcolm X, for whom Hughes's "dream deferred" had really exploded: "No, I'm not an American. . . . So, I'm not standing here speaking to you as an American, or a patriot, or a flag-saluter, or a flag-waver—no, not I. . . . I see America through the eyes of the victim. I do not see any American dream, I see an American nightmare."[9] They have acknowledged, however, with mistrust, that the Stars and Stripes does not sum up their aspirations. I suspect that this attitude also belongs to a movement of a completely different type, namely, the feminist movement of the late 1960s and early 1970s. There is a very marked visual contrast between the demonstrations of the old suffragists at the beginning of the twentieth century and those of the new feminists. The former were as crammed with the national flag as the latter were devoid of it. The contrast might be not casual but political. Just as the former claimed rights of equality and citizenship believed to be inscribed in the country's tradition, so the latter stated principles of gender-based differences that were alien to that tradition. In effect, the feminists were criticizing precisely the "abstract" rights of citizenship and equality of eighteenth-century origin, which they thought had contributed to perpetuating gender inequality, the subordination of women, patriarchy. No Stars and Stripes therefore. There was, nevertheless, a more friendly American symbol, and it was the Statue of Liberty. There is a photograph of a 1970 demonstration at the feet of the statue. Two young women are imitating its posture, with a closed fist instead of a torch and a banner saying, "Women of the World, Unite!"[10]

III **Empire** *Frontiers Old and New*

8 More Stars

The American flag has a feature that I believe to be unique in the panorama of contemporary national flags. It is a flag that changes over time as the national territory changes and increases, and the change and growth are foreseen and regulated by law. The flag is a variable icon geared to automatic expansion, the appropriate emblem of an empire in the making. The idea of empire is incorporated in it from the outset. In effect, before twentieth-century interventions, the only governmental manipulations of the flag had covered precisely this aspect, dating back to the dawn of the republic. If the thirteen stripes and the thirteen stars of 1777 represented the member states, what would have happened if other states had entered the union? In 1794, Congress responded by increasing to fifteen the number of stars and stripes, in recognition of the admission of Vermont and Kentucky. However, the colonization of the West and its political organization in states were proceeding apace; if the flag had been adapted to the new numbers, the accumulation of the stripes would have rendered the design untenable. There was actually great confusion, even in the more official banners. In 1818, someone remarked that, despite the provisions of the Act of 1794, the flag in the entrance hall of Congress still had thirteen stripes, while the one in a nearby barracks already had eighteen (almost as many as the states that there were then), and one in the assembly hall of the House had, for some mysterious reason, only nine. It was, in fact, in 1818 that the legislators adopted the flexible and decisive rule. The stripes went back to being thirteen, the original states, and for the first time it was decided that they had to be horizontal. The entry of each new state would entail the addition of a new star, with effect from the Fourth of July following the date of admission. This automatic mechanism has worked for the century and a half since then.

At the time of the war with Mexico, in 1846–47, there were twenty-nine stars. It was then that the young Walt Whitman rejoiced, announcing that an American victory would provide "more stars" for the flag, "a cluster of new stars," as in fact happened.[1] It was then, among other things, that the artillery and infantry regiments began to carry the national flag into battle, instead of leaving it, as they used to do, in the garrison headquarters. And it was then that the exultant expansionists clearly expressed the idea that the United States was called by divine providence to occupy and populate, with free men—that is, white men—the entire North American continent, perhaps as far as Cuba and Canada. The journalist John O'Sullivan coined, for this idea, the successful term "Manifest Destiny" and clearly summarized the characteristics of the young, white American democracy: a postrevolutionary democracy genuinely radical for the times (which European observers watched with horror or fascination), which manifested an extraordinary driving force. A democracy that had "sympathies on behalf of liberty, universal liberty" and that was hungry for the lands of others, ruthless in its westward march of conquest, contemptuous of peoples different from itself. A democracy that wanted Mexican lands but would have done without their Spanish-Indian inhabitants "of mixed and confused blood"; that would willingly have got rid of the "inferior" race of the black slaves, emancipating them and sending them to Mexico; that wanted the lands of the natives, without the natives. O'Sullivan ventured a bold prediction. Three hundred million Americans were "destined to gather beneath the flutter of the stripes and stars, in the fast hastening year of the Lord 1945!"[2]

At the time of the debates on the new Constitution, in 1787, one of its most strenuous defenders, Alexander Hamilton, argued that a centralized federal government was needed to prevent wars between the states. In Federalist No. 6, Hamilton criticized the "Utopian" conviction that commercial republics (in today's language, we would say capitalist democracies) are peaceful, do not start wars; they do, and how, just like absolute states and monarchies. They do it out of thirst for power, lust for wealth, to impose their supremacy in commerce, to take over other nations' trade without their consent. They do it out of a "desire of equality and safety." They do it because "men are ambitious, vindictive, and rapacious." The postrevolutionary North American states, if they remained independent or semi-independent, would have ended up tearing one another apart. And of course, wrote the most realistic and least sentimental of the Founding Fathers, there is no reason to believe that the Americans will behave otherwise. We must rid ourselves of the "fallacy and extravagance of those idle theories" according to which we would be different from other peoples, free from their imperfections. Is it not, perhaps, time to wake up "from the deceitful dream of a golden age?"; to convince ourselves that we too, like everyone else, "are yet remote from the happy empire of perfect wisdom and perfect virtue?"[3] The creation of the federation prevented the war between the states, at least for seventy years. Nothing, however, prevented the federal republic itself from waging war against its neighbors, the Indian nations and the sister republic of Mexico; and nothing prevented many Americans from convincing themselves that they were living in a happy and virtually perfect empire.

The idea of freedom of the expansionists of the 1840s was a little different from that of the early revolutionaries. For Tom Paine, the American Revolution is the spark of liberation for the whole of humanity; America is the refuge of universal freedom, but it does not have exclusive ownership of it. For O'Sullivan, universal freedom coincides with American freedom: it belongs to America. The idea of freedom had been "nationalized." And the program to extend its compass was selfish and nationalistic. It implied, at one and the same time, freedom for the American nation, freedom for the American state, freedom for the American individual, and therefore, inevitably, it implied extending the borders of the United States.[4] All this could be viewed with mixed feelings, or with indifference, by distant Europe, but it was hardly reassuring for the neighboring states. In 1847, the Mexicans observed with resentment the *yanqui* flag raised by the marines on the beaches of California and of Veracruz and finally on the strongholds of Chapultepec, the so-called Halls of Montezuma that dominate the road to Mexico City ("From the Halls of Montezuma / To the shores of Tripoli" are the opening lines of the hymn of the U.S. Marine Corps, and this certainly does not help its popularity in Central America or, for that matter, in the Arab countries).[5] For decades, the Canadians looked with concern at their southern neighbors who spoke of also freeing them from the British yoke, of giving them U.S. citizenship. As the English novelist Anthony Trollope wrote, precisely from Canada, in 1862, "those who live near [the star-spangled banner], and not under it, fancy that they hear too much of it."[6]

The flag of the United States was even less reassuring for the Native American nations, to which it announced the arrival of a foreign power, aggressive and domineering.[7] The Stars and Stripes did not often appear on the Indian battlefields, though. The U.S. Cavalry was only authorized to use it during the Civil War; once the war was over, and until the turn of the century, it went back to hoisting other banners—blue with the symbols of regiments, bicolor swallow-tailed with the symbols of companies.[8] It was under these banners that the blue soldiers massacred the natives, and it was beside one of these banners that George A. Custer was massacred at Little Bighorn in June 1876. Whatever may be conveyed by quite a few prints of the time, and later by some Hollywood motion pictures, Custer did not fall defending the national flag; that is a patriotic invention, just as it is a romantic invention that would have him, at the supreme moment, with his saber drawn (that day, the 7th Cavalry did not have sabers).[9] In the same patriotic spirit, a riot of Stars and Stripes decorated the Wild West Show of Buffalo Bill, which spectacularly recreated this and other brutal episodes of the white conquest of the continent. Buffalo Bill also staged reconciliation ceremonies between "the White man" and "The Former Foe—Present friend—the *American*." And yet the program included demonstrations of shooting skills entitled "The Rifle as an Aid to Civilization"; "without the rifle ball," it was explained, "we of America would not be to-day in the possession of a free and united country." Later the Wild West Show added to the repertoire the battle of San Juan, fought in Cuba by Teddy Roosevelt's cowboys, during the Spanish-American War of 1898. The saga of the West continued in more exotic settings.[10]

The photograph of Theodore Roosevelt and his men on San Juan Hill, huddled together around the flag that flutters above them, introduces the twentieth century. There is a film of their cavalry charge up the hill, and it could also be a production in the Wild West Show. It is the first filmed war sequence in history, and it was staged: it is the filming of a second charge repeated for the movie cameras, shortly after the first, because the first had not come out well.[11] The war with Spain was fought to help independentist movements against the residue of an old colonial empire. And yet, wherever the U.S. troops arrived, they replaced the Spanish flag with the Stars and Stripes, in Havana as in Puerto Rico and the Philippines. In some cases, the commanders had to order its removal, so as not to irritate the locals. In Manila, Commodore George Dewey destroyed the Spanish fleet in a few hours and, in the chaos that followed, ordered that the largest flag he had should be hoisted on the city garrison; at that precise moment, by chance, or perhaps miraculously, there appeared, amid the chaos, an orderly military band that "saluted the colors as they went up and played the national air."[12] Dewey hoisted an even larger flag, gigantic, five hundred feet long, on his flagship on his triumphant return home. Mystic patriots and enthusiasts spoke of Old Glory as the banner-elect of God, a voice from heaven that manifests itself in distant islands, a missionary presence destined to remain. "We cannot retreat from any soil where Providence has unfurled our banner," said the young senator of Indiana, the Republican Albert Beveridge, in his speech "The March of the Flag": "it is ours to save that soil for Liberty and Civilization."[13]

As a matter of fact, not everyone agreed. The anti-imperialist (Democrat) William Jennings Bryan wanted the national emblem to be lowered as soon as possible, and forever, from the islands just occupied: because, he said, the "mission of that flag is to float—not over a conglomeration of commonwealths and colonies—but over 'the land of the free and the home of the brave.'"[14] Mark Twain was also an anti-imperialist but, being Mark Twain, was more caustic, sharp, offensive. In a speech, he called the American flag in Manila "polluted"; after the ensuing pandemonium, he rectified his statement by saying that it was the American government, which had sent the flag there "in a robbing expedition," that was polluted. In an article, he wrote that the U.S. soldiers involved in repressing in blood the independentist insurgents in the Philippines, were doing "bandit's work under a flag which bandits have been accustomed to fear, not to follow." He proposed a new and more suitable design for the Stars and Stripes, "with the white stripes painted black and the stars replaced by

Empire triumphant 1898 Roosevelt in Cuba. Colonel Roosevelt and his Rough Riders at the top of the hill that they captured. Battle of San Juan, Spanish-American War, July 1, 1898. Photograph by William Dinwiddie. (Prints and Photographs Division, Library of Congress)

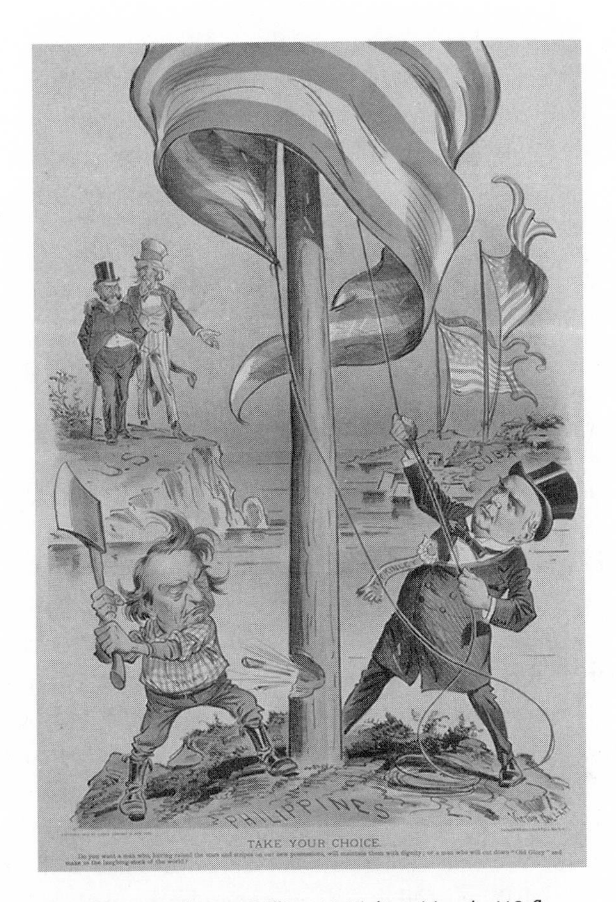

Empire contested 1900 William McKinley raising the U.S. flag in the Philippines, and William Jennings Bryan chopping it down, with U.S. flags flying over Puerto Rico and Cuba. Lithograph, color. (Prints and Photographs Division, Library of Congress)

the skull and cross-bones": a pirates' flag.[15] The same sentiments echo in one of the poems of the *Spoon River Anthology* (1915), in which Edgar Lee Masters gives voice to a young American who enlists to fight against the "barbarous" Filipinos to uphold the honor of the Stars and Stripes and ends up in the rice fields of Manila, where he encounters the real barbarity of all wars, until the final hour:

> To the hour of the charge through the steaming swamp,
> Following the flag,
> Till I fell with a scream, shot through the guts.
> Now there's a flag over me in Spoon River!
> A flag! A flag![16]

In the meantime, the occupation of the continent had been completed. In 1912, New Mexico and Arizona entered the Union, and the stars on the flag became forty-eight. (The last two stars representing Alaska and Hawaii, which brought the total to fifty, were added only in 1959 and 1960.) That the overseas expansion should have begun at that time was not a matter of chance. Of course, everywhere, the first outposts of the presence of the new American power were not its soldiers but the goods of its powerful productive machine. And they too were often associated with the Stars and Stripes, on their brand names, labels, and advertising. The authorities were not too happy about this. In 1905, Congress forbade the use of the national colors in trademarks that had to be registered with the federal Patent Office. Many states also banned their inclusion in advertisements and labels. A 1907 Supreme Court ruling confirmed that this prohibition was right and appropriate because, it said, it is a sign of respect for the beloved symbol of national prestige and honor. These provisions were never implemented, but their very existence testifies to how many people feared that commercialism would pollute the values of patriotism,[17] which seems the ultimate irony for a country that has always been considered the very incarnation of the commercial spirit. My favorite quote on this subject comes from a 1909 Italian magazine that, at the end of a long censure of "this country which does not exist, which is not a people, does not have a name, has no history," that "is a crowd of brash storekeepers under a *corporate name* devoid of all that is not money," declares, if it were to conquer the world, "the world would be a fair whose symbol would be the flag of the United States: a huge advertising billboard."[18]

9 Does the Constitution Follow the Flag?

The 1898 treaty with Spain, which sanctioned the independence of Cuba and the transfer to the United States of Guam, Puerto Rico, and the Philippines, posed an unprecedented dilemma. The nineteenth-century expansion had taken for granted that the territories acquired beyond the original boundaries of 1783—namely, the vast Louisiana, Florida, the Mexican Southwest, and Alaska—would become states of the Union. It was not clear if the Constitution allowed these acquisitions (Thomas Jefferson was convinced that it did not but then changed his mind about Louisiana) or if the creation of new states was a constitutional obligation.[1] However, that is how things went, and the Constitution extended its protection over the whole continent. The idea was, as a federal judge later explained, that the contiguous United States would have been inhabited "only by people of the same race"—white settlers capable of governing themselves according to republican rules—or "by scattered bodies of native Indians," scattered and hence, one imagines, easily marginalized.[2] Puerto Rico and the Philippines were another matter. They were distant islands, "tropical," full of "dark races" considered illiterate, primitive, or semicivilized, incapable of self-government. Nobody wanted these lands to become states and their inhabitants citizens of the United States and therefore joint arbiters of the national destiny. People then wondered if the Constitution should really apply fully and *ex proprio vigore* wherever the Stars and Stripes was flying—that is, using the catchphrase coined by Democratic Senator James K. Jones, "Does the Constitution follow the [national] flag?"[3]—or, on the contrary, if, in some cases, the flag could be a symbol of pure colonial domination.

The issue was the object of intense political and electoral conflicts, of a pitched battle of satirical cartoons,[4] and then, as always, of the attention of the Supreme Court. The political-electoral conflicts reflected party divisions. The Republicans of the wartime president, William McKinley, were mostly imperialists and colonialists. They believed that the Constitution was valid only for the states of the Union; it could be extended to new territories and make them states, but only by a free decision of Congress, if Congress deemed it appropriate. In this case it was not appropriate, and the United States should follow the example of the European powers, namely, by annexing the tropical islands as dependent colonies, with a subordinate status. The federal government had the authority to do so; nothing in the Constitution prevented it. The Democrats of William Jennings Bryan were mostly anti-imperialists or, more precisely, anticolonialists. They accused the Republicans of being dangerous subversives, of being "apostles of the New Evangel"—a "fantastic and wicked scheme of colonial expansion" of the European type that would disrupt the American system of government.[5] They believed that the Constitution born of an anticolonial revolution could not accept colonies, that it would apply automatically to every new territory acquired, at the moment of acquisition, and therefore that the tropical islands would become states and their dark inhabitants American citizens, whether one liked it or not. The Democrats, racists like everyone else, did not like it and proposed getting rid of that embarrassing burden.

It was on this proposal that the Democratic Party staked its fortunes in the 1900 presidential elections. Its electoral platform opened with the usual solemn tributes to the Declaration of Independence and the Constitution; but for once the patriotic paraphrasing of the founding documents did not only have a ritual purpose. The repetition of the principle that governments derive their just powers from the consent of the governed served to affirm that without consent there is tyranny and "that to impose upon any people a government of force is to substitute the methods of imperialism for those of a republic." The appeal to the constitutional language was used to reiterate that "the Constitution follows the flag," that "imperialism abroad will lead quickly and inevitably to despotism at home." Even Republican Abraham Lincoln was recruited to the cause, with the evocative statement that "no nation can long endure half republic and half empire." Starting from these principles, the party condemned the Republican policy as an open violation of the fundamental law and the national tradition, as an attempt "to commit the United States to a colonial policy inconsistent with republican institutions and condemned by the Supreme Court."[6] The Democrats were defeated, and McKinley was reelected. The imperialists won, and the Supreme Court, far from condemning them, hastened to side with them. Because, as observed by Mr. Dooley, the satirical character created by the writer Finley Peter Dunne, "No matter whether th' Constitution follows the flag or not, th' Soopreme Coort follows th' iliction returns."[7]

Within a few years, in a series of rulings known as the Insular Cases, the Supreme Court recognized the legality of colonialism and the territorial limitations to the power of the Constitution. As has often happened in the U.S. commercial polity, such delicate issues were resolved talking about business and taxes. The most important case, *Samuel Downes v. George R. Bidwell* (1901), in fact concerned a New York merchant who refused to pay duty on goods imported from Puerto Rico because, he argued, the Constitution stipulates that "all duties, imposts and excises shall be uniform throughout the United States";[8] therefore, there should not be any customs barriers between the various parts of the country, including overseas conquests. But, in fact, was Puerto Rico part of the United States? Here the Court broadened the scope of the discussion. Taking up the Republicans' legal arguments and everybody's racial beliefs, it asserted that the extension of the Constitution to new territories and the incorporation of new states was a "liberality" on the part of Congress. And Congress had "not only the power to govern such territory, but to prescribe upon what terms the United States will receive its inhabitants, and what their status shall be in what Chief Justice Marshall termed the "American empire." There was no obligation to give them citizenship rights, especially if they were members of "uncivilized" races—"absolutely unfit to receive it." In this particular case, Puerto Rico was not ordained to become a state or its residents to become citizens; it was "a territory appurtenant to and belonging to the United States, but not a part of the United States within the . . . Constitution."[9] It was, in other words, a colony.

The Court's arguments did, in fact, contain some radical disagreements and important qualifications. The judgment was approved by a majority of five to four. Writing a vigorous dissenting opinion for the minority, Justice John M. Harlan objected to the legal logic and political morality of the whole line of reasoning. He took up the arguments of the Democrats and called the colonial idea arbitrary, despotic, monarchical, "wholly inconsistent with the spirit and genius, as well as with the words, of the Constitution." Writing for the majority, Justice Henry B. Brown acknowledged that at least the issue of the personal rights of the colonized was a complicated matter. He distinguished between natural and artificial rights in the Constitution. The natural rights, including freedom of religion and speech, property, the due process of law, immunity against unreasonable searches and seizures, as well as against cruel and unusual punishments, are "fundamental" and nonnegotiable. They do not depend on the discretion of Congress even in the colonies; their residents are protected in "life, liberty and property" (nothing is said about the pursuit of happiness). The artificial rights include citizenship and voting rights and trial by jury; they are "peculiar to our own system of jurisprudence," a product of the Anglo-Saxon tradition, and are not exportable to other peoples, or rather they can be only at the discretion of Congress. In other words, the Bill of Rights did apply, and the right to democratic self-government did not. It is said that Secretary of War Elihu Root summed up the judgment this way: "the Constitution follows the flag, but it does not quite catch up with it." Senator Jones commented, instead, that now the new question was, "*Ought* the Constitution to follow the flag?"[10]

The Insular Cases still regulate the small tropical American empire: Puerto Rico and Guam (the Philippines have been independent since 1946), American Samoa, the U.S. Virgin Islands, the Northern Mariana Islands. Each of these territories is governed in a different way, with extensive local autonomy, but each with provisions dictated by Congress and revocable by Congress. For constitutional purposes, they are not part of the United States, but neither are they foreign; they are, in a delightful linguistic tangle that reflects the institutional muddle, "foreign in a domestic sense." The residents have certain rights, the "fundamental" ones, but not all; for example, they do not vote at federal elections. They live under the Stars and Stripes—but are not members of the U.S. body politic.[11] Such an arrangement is the object of much criticism; a judge has defined it as a residue of the "racist imperialism of a previous era."[12] Other critics have argued that the Constitution should apply fully wherever the United States is sovereign, in law or de facto, in the unincorporated U.S. territories and elsewhere. I sense that a new legal literature is intent on redesigning the "constitutional geography," extending the territorial limits of the effectiveness of the Constitution beyond the national borders. "No human being subject to the governance of the United States should be a stranger to the Constitution" goes the reading.[13] Fair enough, even if this would seem a rather exacting commitment for a country that is an omnipresent global power. Or perhaps it is the ultimate imperial fantasy.

And what about the flag that flutters over the military base of Guantánamo—and that has fluttered long enough over its prisons and prisoners? Hoisted by the Marines on June 12, 1898, it has never been lowered; and it is controversial whether or not it is followed by the Constitution. The Guantánamo Bay Naval Station lives in a sort of limbo. Officially it is not U.S. territory but, rather, Cuban territory ceded on a rental basis; and the lease, signed in 1903 and renewed in 1934, states that "the United States recognizes the continuance of the ultimate sovereignty of the Republic of Cuba." However, the Supreme Court, ruling in *Rasul v. Bush* (2004), took a very matter-of-fact, no-nonsense approach. It decided that the ultimate sovereignty may well belong to Cuba but that the government in Washington has the authority to exercise "complete jurisdiction and control." According to the concurring opinion of Justice Anthony M. Kennedy, history has made Guantánamo "a place that belongs to the United States, extending the 'implied protection' of the United States to it." Whether that involves the full implementation of the Constitution is unclear. What is clear is that the conservatives on the

Court were very alarmed. Justice Antonin Scalia's dissenting opinion described the majority opinion as "irresponsible": "judicial adventurism of the worst sort," because it has granted the enjoyment of important rights to foreigners outside national borders "to the four corners of the earth."[14] The flag is one thing, the Constitution quite another. As constitutional scholar Sanford Levinson has suggested, "If you really start believing that the Constitution follows the flag, then Guantánamo, and for that matter our bases in Afghanistan, really come into play."[15] As do the bases in Iraq, and elsewhere.

10 Iwo Jima

The most famous twentieth-century image of the Stars and Stripes is probably the one of the six marines raising it, on February 23, 1945, on Mount Suribachi on Iwo Jima, the first Japanese island conquered by American forces. It is then a picture of war, of the last phase of the Second World War, shot by Associated Press reporter Joe Rosenthal. The composition is so perfect that it seems staged. In fact it is not, even if the shot does not capture the first flag-raising on the hill but the second, a few hours later, with a larger flag, more visible and symbolically powerful (it came from Pearl Harbor, where it had been recovered from the rubble of the Japanese bombardment on December 7, 1941). The photograph was immediately published by newspapers and periodicals, and it won the Pulitzer Prize. It was displayed in shop windows, discussed in schools. The government circulated it to galvanize Americans and Allies alike in the final war effort and to sell war bonds. Later it used it as the model for the bronze monument known as the U.S. Marine Corps Memorial, or Iwo Jima Memorial, unveiled in 1954 in the Arlington National Cemetery near Washington, D.C. It became, in other words, a revered national icon. The emotional impact of the photograph is, in itself, strong and dramatic: it evokes courage, patriotism, willingness to sacrifice, joint effort, statuesque dynamism, a determined and victorious action. It was even more so in the political and ideological context of its time and of the times that followed, namely, the context of the antifascist war on two fronts, in Europe and Asia, the new international role of the United States, and the incipient Cold War with a new enemy.[1]

Victorious flags of the United States had already been seen abroad, in the course of the century, and had provoked contrasting reactions. As I mentioned in the preceding chapters, they had been seen at the beginning of the twentieth century in Asia and Central America and the

Caribbean, greeted with hostility by locals and with mixed feelings by many Americans. The reception had been the reverse in various parts of Europe, when the Yankees arrived during the First World War to give the French, British, and Italians a helping hand. The colors of the Stars and Stripes fluttered merrily in the streets of Paris. According to enthusiastic eyewitnesses, the red, white, and blue of the American flag blended with the red, white, and blue of the French one, and it was not possible to tell where one ended and the other began (Ah! The two republics! *La fraternité*!). "There is now 'new glory' for Old Glory, the glory of a noble sacrifice that a sister tricolor may float free from the black shadow of the Prussian ensign." In London, the red, white, and blue of the Union Jack also combined with the others in a blaze of "concord among the tricolors," of chromatic and political harmony.[2] In Italy, the national colors were not exactly the same (there was green instead of blue), but nevertheless, the Fourth of July 1918 was celebrated with great euphoria, with the help of a well-oiled propaganda machine. A U.S. official in Rome wrote, "There is an almost pathetic desire on the part of Italians to have one of our flags." And in January 1919, President Wilson was welcomed as a messiah, a saint, with crowds who lit candles in front of his portraits. Of course, Wilson's Italian and European popularity dissolved in the face of the difficulties of the peace talks. And the Americans went back home, or so it seemed.[3]

There was continuity between the policies that brought the flag of the United States to Latin America and then to Europe, a continuity not without its disturbing ironies. In both cases, the doctrine laid down decades earlier, in 1823 by President James Monroe, was evoked. The original Monroe Doctrine was America-centered, antimonarchical, anticolonialist, and overly ambitious. It aimed at defending the republics born from the dissolution of the Spanish Empire in the Americas, at protecting "our southern brethren" from the reactionary designs of the European Holy Alliance. Around 1900, it had become something else, a means of realpolitik, a justification for U.S. imperial designs in the Caribbean. In the same period, however, the Monroe Doctrine had acquired a reach that was no longer continental but rather universal, and on this plane it preserved something of its liberating virginity, subversive of the existing international order. Radical groups used it to voice support for all the peoples who were fighting to win free and republican institutions.[4] And so did Wilson, in January 1917, to give meaning to the peace he had in mind for the postwar period, after the war that should have put an end to all wars. Wilson proposed that nations should adopt "the doctrine of President Monroe as the doctrine of the world: that no nation should seek to extend its polity over any other nation or people, but that every people should be left free to determine its own polity." These are "American principles, American policies," he said, and they are also the ideals and hopes of all mankind: "the principles and policies of forward-looking men and women everywhere, of every modern nation, of every enlightened community." For him, the insularity of the United States was over;

Two empires "Raising the Flag on Iwo Jima," February 23, 1945. Photograph by Joe Rosenthal/ Associated Press. (National Archives and Records Administration)

Two empires Reichstag Red flag, May 2, 1945. Photograph by Red Army photographer Yevgeny Ananievich Khaldei. (Copyright Khaldei/PhotoSoyouz/Mark Grosset Photographies. Prints and Photographs Division, Library of Congress)

the whole world was America, although the world, for the moment, was reluctant to recognize it.[5]

In the second postwar period, the Iwo Jima flag was a triumphant message of liberation and freedom, signaling the end of a nightmare—and the advent of a global power that wanted to extend its influence over all the continents in a way, this time, permanent. It embodied the concept summed up in the midst of the war by General George C. Marshall: "We are determined that before the sun sets on this terrible struggle our flag will be recognized throughout the world as a symbol of freedom on the one hand and of overwhelming force on the other."[6]

That image marked new ideological and imperial borders, east and west. It matched and was in stark contrast with another famous image, the picture of Soviet soldiers raising their own Soviet red flag, on May 2,

1945, over the Berlin Reichstag in ruins (a picture actually shot in imitation of the Iwo Jima one).[7] It was transformed into the spectacular graphics of the posters of the John Wayne flick *Sands of Iwo Jima* (1949), the prototype of the Hollywood Pacific-war films in which the villains are defined mainly in racial terms, as "Nips" or "Japs" or "lemon-colored characters." The Stars and Stripes became the flag of the free world that was opposed to the Communist nonfreedom; it became one of the two flags of the Cold War, not always and not everywhere a bearer of freedom; it became the flag involved in hot wars that flared up almost immediately in Asia, in Korea and Vietnam. It was also the symbol of a vigorous economic expansion and a cultural offensive on the frontier of mass consumption and mass entertainment. The publisher Henry Luce announced it in his article "The American Century" (1941). The United States, wrote Luce, is the most powerful and vital nation on earth, called to play a dominant role, and the instruments of this supremacy are the democratic principles, free enterprise, the free market, prosperity, and not least in importance, "American jazz, Hollywood movies, American slang, American technology and products."[8]

The marines of the Iwo Jima flag-raising were the latest among the many examples of heroic and virtuous masculinity presented by wartime propaganda to young American combatants. The same propaganda, in the meantime, had used the flag to mobilize women, in some ways extolling their traditional roles as family caretakers, in other ways opening the door to unaccustomed opportunities. With men at the front, as in the First World War, women invaded male occupations, even in heavy industry. The messages that pushed them into those uncharted territories invoked, much more than in the First World War, their abilities, strength, "masculine" independence. "We can do it!" they stated in big letters. One of the most striking visual messages was painted by Norman Rockwell for the cover of the *Saturday Evening Post* of May 29, 1943. Standing out, against the background of a large Stars and Stripes, is the monumental figure of Rosie the Riveter, a figure inspired by a successful song of the previous year. In overalls, with her sleeves rolled up on muscular arms, sitting on a stool during her lunch break, Rosie, the factory worker, looks into the distance with a detached and self-assured air and nonchalantly tramples on a copy of Hitler's *Mein Kampf*. Above her head there is the playful canonization of a halo. She is wearing nail varnish and lipstick, but on her broad lap there is a powerful riveting machine, undoubtedly, menacingly phallic. With her somewhat disturbing transgender quality, Rosie the Riveter is no vulnerable Great War–era poster woman whose honor begs to be protected by male warriors. She can take care of herself and can handle the Nazis.[9] Perhaps also because of this depiction, the marines of the film *Sands of Iwo Jima*, filmed when the war was over and with the benefit of hindsight, present themselves as fathers and husbands far from home, who protect the homeland and their homes with the necessary firmness, but who, with the same determination, want to return to their families and take up again their role as breadwinners, before it is too late.

Twenty years after Iwo Jima, in the 1960s, the imperial Stars and Stripes were being burnt in the streets—even in the United States, in the heart of the empire. The increasingly massive military involvement by the U.S. government in the war in Vietnam (once again, as at the beginning of the century, in the Asia rice fields) had given rise to a vigorous domestic opposition movement. In the American streets, the majority of the protesters expressed disappointment and sorrow at their government's choices, the belief that those choices were betraying the country's true values. That is why there were flags carried at half-mast, perhaps accompanied by mocking slogans such as "Drop Acid Not Bombs" (as in a famous 1969 Robert Altman picture). In the same spirit, there were those who claimed that it was necessary to engage in flag cleansing, in the purification of the besmirched, betrayed flag, rather than in flag burning. However, in the most militant protests, the national emblem was burned and sometimes replaced with that of the enemy, the Vietcong flag. They were scandalous acts, which aroused heated discussions among the protesters themselves. Some feared that it was a suicidal practice, alienating the sympathies of those they wanted to convert to the cause, for example, the working class, which precisely by those acts felt insulted in its patriotism. Many working-class neighborhoods were in fact decorated with flags in support of the war, and there were prowar union rallies and bitter strife with antiwar radicals. The flags insulted by middle-class radicals stood also in dramatic contrast with those that draped the coffins of the dead soldiers brought back home, who were mainly sons of the working class. A few protesters, however, believed that flag burning was the right way to express a total rejection of the imperialist nature of the country or, for those who were the least revolutionary among them, that it was part of an established tradition of dissent against an unjust government.[10]

Burning or otherwise profaning a symbol is, like honoring it, the act of those who recognize its power. It does not mean that the symbol is actually hated in itself; one can love it and hate the use to which others put it. The American tradition of radical dissent moves in this direction, a direction pointed to in the nineteenth century by Henry David Thoreau in *Civil Disobedience*, the pamphlet he wrote against the war with Mexico of 1846–47. There are those, and they are the majority, said Thoreau, who serve the state as machines, without exercising any free ethical judgment, as if they were stones, pieces of wood, horses and dogs. They are generally considered good citizens. Take a marine: "such a man as an American government can make, or such as it can make a man with its black arts—a mere shadow and reminiscence of humanity, a man laid out alive and standing, and already, as one may say, buried under arms with funeral accompaniments." Then there are very few others, "heroes, patriots, martyrs, reformers in the great sense, and *men* [who] serve the state with their consciences also, and so necessarily resist it for the most part; and they are commonly treated as enemies by it." When it is necessary, when the state becomes an agent of injustice, these people should disobey, break the law, throw their bodies in the gears of the state machine to stop it. The fact that they are a minority cannot prevent them from acting, said Thoreau: "I think that it is enough if they have God on their side," without waiting for anything or anyone else.[11] The appeal to God or to the sanctity of individual conscience is very problematic in a

Bitter fruits Photos of loved ones left at the Vietnam War Memorial in Washington, D.C. (GNU Free Documentation License, Free Software Foundation)

democracy, based on majority rule. And yet it sanctifies the practices of resistance. It certifies that the true patriots resist the state, that, as one slogan says, "patriots who love America burn flags."[12]

The conflict over Vietnam did not subside with the conclusion of the war. It continued and became a conflict over memory. How should a controversial war be commemorated, a war that divided the country, a war never officially declared, a war that was lost? The clash became bitter and institutional when it came to erecting a monument to the fallen in Washington, D.C.—and ended with the construction of two separate monuments. The first monument, unveiled in 1982, consists of two black granite walls that intersect to form a wide V embedded in the ground. There are no national symbols or references to collective ideals. The names of the fifty-eight thousand soldiers who died are carved in the stone, one by one, in alphabetical order year by year. Each name calls for individual and private compassion and grief. Just as individual and private are the small flags left by visitors at the foot of the wall or put precariously in its cracks—left there, every day, by friends and relatives together with personal souvenirs, letters, photographs, cherished objects. Many veterans, however, were dissatisfied with the result, which they saw as a testimony to grief without glory or patriotism, a lugubrious "mass grave" that was silent about the heroism of the dead and the living. They obtained the addition, in 1984, of a second monument, a heroic hyperrealist bronze statue of three soldiers and a large Stars and Stripes. The dedication to the flag, however, is not serene; it refers to principles of freedom defended "in difficult circumstances." And the statue seems, to me, hardly at all heroic; the soldiers are tired and thoughtful and look at the long black wall of their dead companions. Someone had demanded that the Vietnam Veterans Memorial resemble in spirit the Iwo Jima Memorial, but those times and that spirit were far distant.[13] The Vietnam monument's official website stated,

> The Vietnam Veterans Memorial serves as a testament to the sacrifice of American military personnel during one of this nation's least popular wars. The purpose of this memorial is to separate the issue of the sacrifices of the veterans from the U.S. policy in the war, thereby creating a venue for reconciliation.[14]

11 Moon Landing

On July 20, 1969, a rather small (3 × 5 ft.), nylon Stars and Stripes was planted on the lunar surface, in the Sea of Tranquility, by Neil A. Armstrong and Edwin E. "Buzz" Aldrin. The two astronauts, along with Michael Collins, who remained in orbit around the moon, formed the crew of the Apollo 11 mission, the first to bring human beings on to the planet Earth's satellite. The flag ceremony lasted about ten minutes, was photographed by the astronauts themselves, and was broadcast live on television. It marked the spectacular culmination of the ambitious project launched by President John F. Kennedy in May 1961, and it was to be followed by six more lunar expeditions. After Apollo 17, in 1972, the program was canceled; it had, by then, become too costly for a country that, beset by economic, political, and social crises, had to reassess its ambitions, come to terms with a sense of proportion, in heaven as on earth. But in that summer of 1969, the message was clear, a message of success and national pride sent to the whole world that was willing to watch. And yet, behind that flag-raising, there were also concerns and controversies. The colors of the U.S. flag had already been in space. They adorned missiles, orbital spacecraft, lunar probes, astronauts' coveralls. Edward H. White, the first American to walk in space in 1965, had had to buy his own flag patches to put on his coveralls, but after that the National Aeronautics and Space Administration (NASA) adopted them as part of standard clothing. Planting a real flag on the lunar surface was, however, another matter, which had much stronger meanings and implications.

The Apollo project had a predominantly political purpose; it was a grand gesture of Cold War, an episode of the global competition with the Soviet Union. It was for this reason that it managed to garner the enormous resources that it needed. It was, moreover, conceived as an intensely national project, explicitly excluding, from the outset, the scientific and financial involvement of friends and allies, actually refusing any such suggestion. It had to mark the United States' regaining of scientific and technological superiority, which seemed compromised after the Soviet space successes, from the first Sputnik (1957) to the first orbital flight of Yuri Gagarin (April 1961). It was right after Gagarin's spectacular flight that President Kennedy announced the launch of the lunar adventure. He also announced that it would be an all-American, Stars-and-Stripes adventure. He made it eloquently clear on several occasions, among them the speech given at Rice University in Houston, Texas, on September 12, 1962. We are entering the Space Age, said Kennedy, and we want to be part of it; in fact, we want to lead it:

> For the eyes of the world now look into space, to the moon and to the planets beyond, and we have vowed that we shall not see it governed by a hostile flag of conquest, but by a banner of freedom and peace. We have vowed that we shall not see space filled with weapons of mass destruction, but with instruments of knowledge and understanding. Yet the vows of this Nation can only be fulfilled if we in this Nation are first, and, therefore, we intend to be first.[1]

Kennedy's reference to a hostile flag was not just metaphorical. Three years earlier, on September 13, 1959, the Soviet probe Lunik 2 had struck the surface of the moon (the first terrestrial object to land there), taking with it the red banner with the hammer and sickle of the USSR. The U.S. government became nervous, and it hastened to clarify that it was not enough to "stick a Red flag in the ground" to advance claims on the moon. The nervousness became irritation when, three days later, Nikita Khrushchev arrived in Washington on an official visit. With great media fanfare, Khrushchev brought as a gift to President Dwight Eisenhower a replica of the banner that had landed on the moon.[2] During the welcoming ceremonies, in front of Eisenhower, surrounded by journalists and cameras, Khrushchev said with mischievous magnanimity and a sugary tone,

> We entertain no doubt that the splendid scientists, engineers, and workers of the United States of America who are engaged in the field of conquering Cosmos will also carry their flag to the moon. The Soviet flag, as an old resident of the moon, will welcome your pennant and they will live there together in peace and friendship as we both should live together on the earth in peace and friendship.[3]

On the eve of the flag-decked Apollo 11 moon landing, history repeated itself. In May 1969, the Soviets landed two capsules on Venus (the first terrestrial objects to get there); and they contained, in addition to the obvious scientific instruments, a medallion with the emblem of the USSR and a bas-relief portrait of Lenin. Playing the game of symbolic national politics seemed a necessity for everyone.

On the other hand, had this not always been the case? "It's a characteristic of previous explorations, to plant a symbol upon arriving at a new shore," the astronaut Buzz Aldrin recalled later. "I certainly felt that the American flag is what belonged there."[4] But it was precisely this allusion to possible historical precedents that worried many people. In the 1950s, the comparison between space exploration and the geographical exploration conducted in the past by European colonial powers had been discussed by legal experts. Outer space did not come under the sovereignty of any known—that is, earthly—state; it was, therefore, considered open to discovery and conquest by anyone who had the strength and capability of doing so, perhaps by means of the old legal criteria of territorial appropriation and the old rituals (indeed, by planting a banner). This "colonial" hypothesis was finally rejected, and the rejection was sanctioned by the United Nations. The Outer Space Treaty of 1967 was the first of a series of agreements on the exploration and peaceful, nonacquisitive use of space promoted by the United Nations. It stipulated, in article 2, that "outer space, including the Moon and other celestial bodies, is not subject to national appropriation by claim of sovereignty, by means of occupation, or by any other means."[5] Taking one's own flag to the moon, therefore, could no longer, in any way, mean claiming sovereignty over it. Such a claim, in fact, had never been advanced, not even by the Soviet Union on the basis of the 1959 episode, well before the treaty had been conceived. From the point of view of international law, the colonial paradigm was banned.

And yet that paradigm persisted, as an undercurrent, in the American public discourse. The space enterprise was launched with the Kennedy rhetoric of the New Frontier, and historically the frontier had been an advancing line of colonization, a mobile front of wars of conquest against native populations. It was then mentioned by Ronald Reagan in perfect continuity with the winning of the West. In a speech given on June 14, 1985, Flag Day, Reagan repeated, "From the mountains of Kentucky to

New frontiers Buzz Aldrin and the U.S. flag on the moon, July 1969. Astronaut Edwin E. Aldrin, Jr., poses for a photograph beside the deployed flag of the United States during the Apollo 11 extravehicular activity. The Lunar Module is on the left. (National Aeronautics and Space Administration)

New frontiers Jeronimo Suñol, 1894, bronze sculpture of Christopher Columbus, Central Park, New York. (Copyright Keith Maguire)

the shores of California to the Sea of Tranquility on the Moon, our pioneers carried our flag before them, a symbol of the indomitable spirit of a free people."[6] The flag held by the astronauts in the famous NASA photographs obviously evoked the image, so often repeated in prints and open-air statues, of a Christopher Columbus who takes possession of other people's lands in the name of a distant monarch; in fact, it reminds of that precursor in the posture of the figures, the composition of the frame, the focus on the banner. This evocation did not please everyone, in the heated atmosphere of the Sixties. As the *New York Times* of July 4, 1969, reminded its readers, to some Americans the flag was a source of thrill and patriotic emotion, but to others—for instance, some black people—it was a threat.[7] On the moon there were no colored natives to civilize or deport, by fair means or foul, but earthly racial tensions extended up there. The African American painter and performer Faith Ringgold offered her own *Flag for the Moon* (1969). The painting depicts a flag, on which, behind the stars, one can make out the word "die," and the stripes, black instead of white, are arranged to form the word "nigger." "Die Nigger" was the message of anger to be launched beyond the sky.[8]

It was not only a question of the anger of Sixties radicals, black and white. A very authoritative official such as Roger Launius, the NASA chief historian and later head of the Space History Division of the Air and Space Museum in Washington, D.C. (the man who would have liked "to be the first historian into space"), recalled how even in establishment circles "there were people at the time, and have been people since then, who thought that planting any flag up there was a bad idea." And he explained why: "After the fifteenth century when Europe was pushing outward, the Europeans were planting flags all over the place and claiming the territory for their home countries. They thought that set a bad precedent."[9] Liberal observers, both inside and outside NASA, suggested that the astronauts should leave on the moon, along with the Stars and Stripes, the symbol of international cooperation, the flag of the United Nations.[10] But the House of Representatives strongly objected. It approved a nationalist resolution that underlined that the Apollo project was funded with American taxpayers' money; the space agency therefore had to use "our flag, Old Glory"—and only that—"as a symbol of U.S. preeminence in space to which the citizens of this Nation can refer with pride." Bowing to the provisions of the Outer Space Treaty, the resolution specified that this "was intended as a symbolic gesture of national pride in achievement and was not to be construed as a declaration of national appropriation by claim of sovereignty."[11]

NASA moved with great bureaucratic wisdom and skill. In February 1969, it appointed a Committee on Symbolic Activities for the First Lunar Landing, to weigh the technical options (not to hinder the mission, not to create unnecessary hazards) and the political ones.[12] The idea of the UN flag was considered and set aside, because of the House resolution. The idea of a set of small flags of the whole world was considered and rejected, for the same reason. The national flag was to remain by itself. And yet the committee devised some communication strategies to play down the nationalist impact and the colonial implications; to do so, it used the language of American universalism, of America as the representative and interpreter of the whole of humanity. The event, it explained, was to be represented "as an historic step forward of all mankind that has been accomplished by the United States." In fact, the name of the country was not much trumpeted about. The commemorative plaque left in the Sea of Tranquility did not contain the image of the Stars and Stripes, as envisaged at the outset, but the stylized profile of the two terrestrial hemispheres. And the inscription does not mention directly the United States: "Here men from the planet Earth first set foot upon the moon July 1969, AD. We came in peace for all mankind." The words Armstrong uttered in the fateful moment—"That's one small step for [a] man, one giant leap for mankind."—were thought in the same spirit. Buzz Aldrin, as always, was the most inspired. In an article for the weekly magazine *Life*, he wrote that, while looking at the flag, he felt an "almost mystical unification of all people in the world at that moment."[13]

At that mystical moment, there were some technical difficulties. The machinery for the lunar flag-raising had been planned in detail so that it would be light and strong, take up little room, be easy to operate by the astronauts in their encumbering spacesuits, and finally make a good impression in an environment with no atmosphere and no wind. To resolve this last problem, crucial for the success of the spectacle, a horizontal telescopic rod had been added to the flag's vertical mast so that, when extended, it would keep the flag totally unfurled. In actual fact, everything did not go smoothly. The vertical mast only penetrated a little in the hard lunar soil; it was rotated several times, and this gave the flag a rotatory motion that, without the friction of the air to stop it, lasted a long time. The horizontal telescopic rod did not open completely, and the fabric of the Stars and Stripes remained crumpled, giving the illusion that it was fluttering. These flaws of the operation, this flag that, in the photographs and video recordings, seems to be fluttering in a breeze that there should not be, have become, to some of the many conspiracy theorists of the world, the main evidence to show that the moon landing never happened, that the event was staged in a television studio on Mother Earth, that the U.S. government contrived everything—and, of course, that the Soviets were in agreement: they knew that the Americans were lying but kept quiet because their space missions were also bogus; they were only annoyed that they had not thought of it first, the biggest and most prestigious lie of them all. This thought seems, after all, rather reassuring: the Cold War was just a game.

IV **Patriots and Dissenters** *Who Owns the Flag?*

12 Desecration

The political conflict over the war in Vietnam, and over imperial policies, continued in another area, that of the use and abuse of the Stars and Stripes. And it became a judicial-political conflict that, once again, reached the Supreme Court—with tangled developments and courtroom drama as gripping as those of a legal thriller.[1] At the height of the protests against the Vietnam War in the late 1960s, state governments began to prosecute acts of desecration of the Stars and Stripes. They did so on the basis of old laws adopted by all the states between 1897 and 1932, and of new laws revised and updated to reflect the new circumstances. After a flag-burning incident in Central Park, in New York City, Congress also added its voice to the chorus and for the first time approved a federal law in this regard, the Flag Desecration Act of 1968. The new rules had a common feature that distinguished them from the old ones. The word *desecration* had entered common parlance at the end of the nineteenth century, when the flag began to be perceived as something sacred. For the devotees of the flag then, however, the list of the desecrators began with the businessmen who exploited the national colors for sordid and antipatriotic—that is commercial—purposes. Only gradually, around the time of the Great War, were they replaced at the top of the list by subversive and un-American radical agitators. The early-twentieth-century legislators were in line with those sentiments and banned all unorthodox uses of the flag, including advertising. The legislators of the 1960s were less sentimental. They deleted the references to commercial desecration and only censured acts of political dissent. The federal act of 1968 provided for fines of up to a thousand dollars and up to a year's imprisonment for anyone who "knowingly casts contempt upon any flag of the United States by publicly mutilating, defacing, defiling, burning, or trampling upon it."[2]

The legal cases all arose from violations of state laws. There were arrests, indictments, and convictions for having burned the flag, defaced it with writing or drawings, or worn it in an improper and derisory manner, sewn on shirts, vests, jeans, perhaps on the backside. Those who were indicted were left-wing militants, pacifists, hippies. The prowar demonstrators also often used the flag inappropriately, as did the very policemen who made the arrests: they had nonregulation flag patches on their uniforms, nonregulation transfer prints on their police cars, Stars-and-Stripes bumper stickers that said, "America, love it or leave it." But this was not desecration; it was not contempt. A case that reached the Supreme Court was that of a student from Seattle, Washington, convicted for having superimposed on the Stars and Stripes the peace symbol (a kind of inverted trident in a circle). In the ruling *Spence v. Washington* (1974), the Supreme Court declared the student's conviction null and void, because it clashed with the First Amendment to the Constitution. With great circumspection, and referring to previous decisions of the Court, the ruling proposed a twofold reasoning. In the first place, it said, the flag as a national symbol "is capable of simultaneously conveying a spectrum of meanings," and all are equally legitimate. Second, the use of the flag to express these meanings is a form of symbolic language, and symbolic speech is also protected by the First Amendment as an extension of the protection accorded, in the text, to the freedom of speech and of the press. Clearly, by handling the flag, the student intended to communicate his own idea of America, and that is his right.[3]

The idea about America that the student wanted to communicate fell into the logic of the American jeremiad. "I felt there had been so much killing and that this was not what America stood for," he said in court. "I felt that the flag stood for America and I wanted people to know that I thought America stood for peace." I stress this fact because the next case the Supreme Court had to deal with on this issue, fifteen years later, arose from gestures and motives far more radical and certainly more repellent to the judges. The result, however, was the same, in fact more dramatic and sensational because it concerned a flag-burning incident. Those who burnt the Stars and Stripes in Dallas in 1984, during the Republican National Convention that marked the apotheosis of President Ronald Reagan, were not disillusioned lovers of America. They were Maoists, members of the Revolutionary Communist Party (RCP). They were supporters, at least in words, of overthrowing the state through armed struggle. Their slogans were "Red, white, and blue, we spit on you" and a more ecumenical "Fuck You, America." The accused in the trials that followed, Gregory Lee Johnson, said that the flag is a symbol of "an imperialist system which dominates and exploits large sections of the world." In the courtrooms of Texas, he stated that he had no love for the system or its flag, and he appeared wearing the T-shirt of his party, with the design of a man brandishing a rifle. Although he declared that he was not a civil libertarian (after the revolution, he would have denied freedom of speech to racists—and to several others), he was defended by lawyers from the American Civil Liberties Union. When his case finally reached the Supreme Court, at the end of 1988, he enlisted the services of William Kunstler, a lawyer of the Center for Constitutional Rights and a true star who had built his career on high-profile trials of this type.

The stage was set for a first-class show. And there certainly was a show, in what a journalist called a heated public debate on the sanctity of the flag. The wording of the judgment *Texas v. Johnson*, issued by the Supreme Court in June 1989, suggested that even behind the scenes, in the august chambers, there had been sparks. The decision was reached with a narrow majority, five to four, and the minority judges attached vigorous dissenting opinions. The opinion of the majority, drawn up by Justice William J. Brennan, was straightforward. Taking up the wording of *Spence v. Washington*, it argued that burning the flag is also symbolic speech and therefore is a right guaranteed by the First Amendment; the laws that punish it are unconstitutional. As a corollary of this statement, there are incisive words: "If there is a bedrock principle underlying the First Amendment, it is that the government may not prohibit the expression of an idea simply because society finds the idea itself offensive or disagreeable." There are surprising words: even the Founding Fathers "were not known for their reverence for the Union Jack." There are finally words of faith in the flag and its thaumaturgic republican qualities, capable of saving everyone, even those who spit on it: "We are tempted to say, in fact, that the flag's deservedly cherished place in our community will be strengthened, not weakened, by our holding today." And, "We do not consecrate the flag by punishing its desecration, for in doing so we dilute the freedom that this cherished emblem represents." And better still, "It is poignant but fundamental that the flag protects those who hold it in contempt"—including the unpleasant Mr. Gregory Lee Johnson.[4]

The dissenting opinions were equally impassioned and more crammed with historical-political considerations than legal ones. That of Justice William Rehnquist was the most authoritative. It came from the chief justice, appointed three years earlier by President Reagan to lead a conservative shift in the Court and now in the minority. Rehnquist traced the history of the Stars and Stripes to show that it occupies a unique place in the life of the nation and therefore deserves special respect, a respect that the government has the authority to require by law. It is not a question of freedom of speech, said Rehnquist, because the flag does not represent "the views of any particular political party [or] any particular political philosophy"; it is not "simply another 'idea' or 'point of view' competing for recognition in the marketplace of ideas." It is rather the object of "an almost mystical reverence" on the part of millions of Americans of every political and philosophical conviction. Justice John Paul Stevens's dissenting opinion had an even broader compass, universal, truly imperial. A flag, said Stevens, is the symbol not only of a nation but also of the ideas that characterize its history and that may be more important than the nation itself. The banner of the United States is the proud symbol not only of thirteen former colonies that have become a great power but also "of freedom, of equal opportunity, of religious tolerance, and of good will for other peoples who share our aspirations." It is a "message to dissidents" throughout the world, who perhaps are not interested in the vicissitudes of the American nation but very interested in the ideas that it champions. Also for them (it should be remembered that these words were written at the beginning of the fateful year 1989, on the eve of the fall of the Berlin Wall), the flag should be protected from those who insult and burn it.

Congress and President George H. W. Bush did not appreciate the decision. With an act of defiance, the legislators almost unanimously approved a federal law that followed the pattern of the 1968 law, de facto nullified by *Texas v. Johnson*. The Flag Protection Act of 1989 added to the crimes against the flag that of laying it out on the floor, and I will explain why in the next chapter. A challenge calls forth another challenge, and as soon as the law came into force, a few hundred people, including the notorious and tireless Gregory Lee Johnson, burnt flags in various parts of the country. Some of them were denounced, and the case went back to the Supreme Court. It was in fact what the government wanted. The Department of Justice, represented by U.S. Solicitor General Kenneth Starr (of later fame as an investigator of Bill Clinton's sex life), asked the judges to reconsider and disavow their earlier judgment. Congressional leaders asked the same thing, arguing that it was the will of the people. The Court replied with the ruling *United States v. Eichman* (June 1990). By the same majority of five to four, with an opinion written by the same Justice Brennan, it also overrode the new Flag Protection Act. And it did so with a tone that seems sharp and irritated. Brennan wrote,

> We decline the Government's invitation to reassess [our previous] conclusion in light of Congress' recent recognition of a purported "national consensus" favoring a prohibition on flag burning. Even assuming such a consensus exists, any suggestion that the Government's interest in suppressing speech becomes more weighty as popular opposition to that speech grows is foreign to the First Amendment.[5]

The story does not end there. Public reactions to the rulings of 1989 and 1990 were among the most inflamed, immediate, and negative in the entire history of the Supreme Court. There were headlines in the media, a storm of letters of protest, rallies, insults to the judges. For some time it seemed that flag burning constituted the main danger for the country. "What in God's name is going on?" a congressman asked; there are no limits anymore: "Are they going to allow fornication in Times Square at high noon?"[6] President Bush launched a campaign to introduce an amendment to the Constitution that would explicitly give Congress the power to prohibit the physical desecration of the flag. He did so as early as 1989, during a very flag-decked ceremony, while thousands of supporters sang the national anthem—where, if not at the Iwo Jima Memorial? Since then, the campaign has continued, without much success. The procedure to amend the Constitution is complex, and the text has never got past the first phase, the approval by a two-thirds majority in both congressional chambers; several times it has been approved by the House and then ignored or dismissed, sometimes narrowly dismissed, by the Senate.[7] Not even the patriotic fervor following September 11 really achieved anything. Opponents of the measure took refuge in defending the sacred purity of the First Amendment. In 2006, U.S. Senator Daniel Inouye, a Hawaii Democrat who won the Medal of Honor for his service in the Second World War, announced his vote against the desecration amendment, stating, "I believe Americans gave their lives in many wars to make certain all Americans have a right to express themselves, even those who harbor hateful thoughts."[8] The then-senator from Illinois, Barack Obama, concurred, quoting from a Vietnam veteran: "Those who would burn the flag destroy the symbol of freedom, but amending the Constitution would destroy part of freedom itself."[9] On the other hand, the main sponsor of the amendment in the House, California Republican Randy Cunningham, a gentleman who was so enthusiastic that he declared, "I'm not proposing this, but in the Civil War it was a penalty of death to desecrate the flag," in 2005 pleaded guilty to taking millions in bribes from defense contractors. He resigned from Congress and was sentenced—not to death but to eight years and four months in prison.[10]

13 Patriotic Pop

The opponents of the antidesecration constitutional amendment often stressed the threat that it could pose to artists' freedom of expression. As early as 1989, while the Supreme Court was considering the *Texas v. Johnson* ruling, a group of painters wrote an appeal to the justices inviting them to speak out against the antidesecration laws; they otherwise feared having to censor their own work. At first sight, this concern seems to be unwarranted. Is not the flag the most *revered* and *celebrated* image in the country's visual arts, both in high culture and the mass cultural industry? That is how it was at the end of the nineteenth century. And the twentieth century also began in grand style. In the early years of that century, during the First World War, the flag became the subject of an extraordinary series of impressionist paintings by Childe Hassam, in which the Stars and Stripes appear bright and cheerful in the streets of New York.[1] The flag triumphantly became a part of Broadway posters, thanks to the musical comedies of George M. Cohan—the author of memorable quips ("Many a bum show is saved by the American flag") and memorable patriotic marches ("You're a Grand Old Flag," 1906), later immortalized in the song "That's Entertainment" (1953):

> The gag may be waving the flag,
> That began, back with Mr. Cohan,
> Hip Hooray! The American Way!
>
> —*That's Entertainment!*[2]

It was in the second half of the twentieth century that something changed. In high culture as well as in popular culture, the flag remained omnipresent, but it became an ambiguous and disputed object, the subject of tormented love-hate affairs. Its representations often acquired critical features, sometimes disrespectful and even insulting, that they did not have before. A romance had come to an end; a fissure had opened between the national iconic universe and important groups of intellectuals and cultural entrepreneurs. As public disputes exploded, they became intertwined with the political and social conflicts of the period. At the aesthetic origins of this rift is a signatory of the artists' appeal of 1989, Jasper Johns.[3]

Johns was one of the founders of Pop Art, and his founding contribution was precisely the flags he painted from 1954 onward and exhibited in the Leo Castelli Gallery in Manhattan. In these paintings, he reproduces the Stars and Stripes as pure abstraction, with dense brush strokes and arbitrary chromatic variations, in some cases only differing shades of white or gray. And the flags are flat, devoid of context, emotion, aura; they do not flutter heroically or patriotically. They want to be viewed with coldness and irony, not with deference. Johns did to the flags what other

Improper ways to display the flag Jasper Johns, *Flag*, 1954–55. Encaustic, oil, and collage on fabric mounted on plywood. (Copyright Jasper Johns. Museum of Modern Art, New York City)

Improper ways to display the flag Abbie Hoffman at the opening of the People's Flag Show, Judson Church, New York, November 9, 1970. (Photo copyright Jan van Raay)

exponents of Pop Art, around 1960, had done with the most popular commercial icons, what Andy Warhol did with his screen-printed Campbell's soup cans and Coca-Cola bottles, Claes Oldenburg with his plaster ice creams and hamburgers, Robert Rauschenberg with his bronze cans of beer: he turned them into aesthetic products. If one observes Johns's flags closely, they reveal even more aspects. They are painted on a collage of newspapers, and headlines and press-cuttings appear through a soft and waxy surface. Are they perhaps suggesting that under the simplicity of the national emblem there are complicated stories and lives, that the nation cannot be encapsulated in a single symbol? The first critics who saw Johns's flags wondered if they were superficial or profound, blasphemous or respectful, or declarations of unrequited love. The first buyers wondered if it was appropriate to accept them in museums, if they would not offend some people's sensibilities. There were debates of this type among the curators of the New York Museum of Modern Art. The flags were finally accepted; in fact, they became advertising mediums for the museums, printed on posters, postcards, mouse pads, whatever. They also became the last resort, or the fig leaf, of ambivalent and blasé patriotism. They are used by those who want to join in some national patriotic solidarity, but with a certain tone, a certain distance.[4]

Johns legitimized the deconsecration of the flag and opened the way for more radical aesthetic and political exercises, angrier or perhaps only more picturesque. The spirit of Pop Art inspired, at the end of the 1960s, radical activists intent on exploiting the mass media, such as Abbie Hoffman and Jerry Rubin—organizers of protests and guerrilla theater events, founders of a Youth International Party that aimed at being a politicized successor of the hippies (the politics of sex, drugs, and rock-'n'-roll). Because of their "subversive" enterprises, they were summoned by the already declining House Committee on Un-American Activities, which, on account of its intervention, lost further prestige. Rubin appeared in the uniform of George Washington's revolutionary army, and stoned out of his mind on hashish. Hoffman arrived wearing a Stars-and-Stripes shirt, bought in a shirt store and therefore legitimately for sale (and I have to say, alas, made in France), and was arrested and convicted for doing so. Wearing the same flag shirt, in 1970 Hoffman participated in a television talk show, and his image was electronically obscured.[5] The flag reappeared on Broadway in the hippylike musical *Hair*, with sneers that would have been inconceivable in the days of old Cohan. In fact, there is the song,

> Don't put it down
> Best one around
> Crazy for the Red Blue and White.

But then it ends with the call to "Com'on watch us burn it at the Be-In."[6] Was it once again a case of love and anger, of disappointed appeals to the country's original values? In 1969, at the Woodstock Festival, Jimi Hendrix performed, with his Fender Stratocaster electric guitar, an acid and distorted version of "The Star-Spangled Banner." For the first time, a pop artist was taking liberties with the national anthem, and he explained why:

> When it was written, it was played in a very beautiful state, you know? Nice and inspiring, you know? Your heart throbs and you say "Great, I'm American" but nowadays, we play it the way the air is in America today. The air is slightly static, isn't it? You know what I mean?[7]

The air was static indeed. In November 1970, with the by-then-famous flag shirt, Hoffman opened, in a Greenwich Village church, a collective monothematic show on the flag, entitled "People's Flag Show." The people, said the Reverend Howard Moody in the presentation, must regain possession of the Stars and Stripes through its artists; bigoted patriots have captured it, betrayed it, made it an instrument for their aggressive policies. The general background was that of the movement against the war in Vietnam. A few months earlier, President Richard Nixon had ordered the invasion of Cambodia; on the campus of Kent State University, in Ohio, the National Guard had fired on the demonstrators, killing four students. But there was also a more specific context, the concern of the New York artistic community for the legal problems facing a gallery owner who had exhibited works deemed offensive to the flag itself (for example, an enormous cloth phallus—with the Stars-and-Stripes pattern). The most provocative event of the exhibition was a ritual flag burning, a happening staged by the Guerrilla Art Action Group. But the most controversial artwork presented was an installation in which the American flag was stuffed into a toilet basin in a wooden cage; and the title was *The American Dream Goes to Pot.* The artist was a young woman named Kate Millett, who had just published her doctoral dissertation, turning it into a feminist best-seller, *Sexual Politics.* Interviewed many years later, Millett explained her intentions and those of her companions: the flag is the symbol of the country, "but it had been degraded by the policy of the war." "We felt in protesting a dishonorable war that we were acting as patriots."[8] The authorities were not appreciative of this form of patriotism. Within a week, Millet's piece was arrested (or rather, it was photographed, and the photograph was arrested—whatever that means), the show was shut down, and three of the organizers were indicted.

One of those indicted was the African American artist Faith Ringgold. The image of the flag had also entered the repertoire of the Black Arts Movement, and it remained there. The work of these artists sprang from white Pop Art, but with a difference. After Johns had freed the national emblem from its historical-patriotic context, black painters and performers such as Ringgold and David Hammons could move in the opposite direction: reassociate it with unusual and controversial historical contexts, relate it, in an ironic or dramatic way, with African American history. Ringgold has repeatedly presented blacks and whites, men and women, as prisoners of the stripes of the flag, and the stripes are dripping with blood (*The Flag Is Bleeding,* 1967 and 1997). To commemorate the bicentenary of the Bill of Rights, she proposed *Freedom of Speech* (1991), a flag crammed with the names of Americans who had to fight for their free-speech right or to whom it had been denied. Hammons has painted, against backgrounds of stars and stripes, black men and women tied and gagged and various *African-American Flags* with black stripes and black stars on a green background, the colors of black nationalism. In 1988, when Jesse Jackson ran for the Democratic presidential nomination, and there were sarcastic comments on the improbability of his attempt, Hammons prepared an installation: a portrait of Jackson, with the colors of his African body modified (pink skin, blue eyes, blond hair and moustache), with a large flag next to him, asks mockingly, *How Ya Like Me Now?* (1988).[9] "The flag is the only true subversive and revolutionary abstraction one can paint," Ringgold has said. And Hammons: "I do not know whether it's the black skin against the bright colors or the irony of the flag being held by an oppressed people. I do use the flag for some kind of shock value."[10]

There was certainly shock value in the installation entitled *What Is the Proper Way to Display the U.S. Flag?* presented by black student "Dread" Scott Tyler at the Art Institute of Chicago, in February 1989. The work consists of a collage of photographs of flag burnings and coffins wrapped in the flag. The collage is hung on the wall, and underneath it is a shelf with an exercise book and pencil; visitors are invited to write their answers to the question of the title. A Stars and Stripes serves as a carpet in front of the shelf; in order to write, one is forced to tread on it and therefore desecrate it or to avoid it with some contortions. It was mainly groups of war veterans who were infuriated. Thousands of them demonstrated in front of the museum, denouncing the directors. Some wore T-shirts with the flag and the inscription, "Burn this, asshole." Others performed actions that turned out to be aesthetically and intellectually very rewarding for Tyler and the more sophisticated observers. Every day, they entered the exhibition, picked up the flag, folded it ceremoniously, put it back on the shelf; they tidied up where the artist had created disorder and gave a possible answer to his provocative question. Every day, other visitors, or museum officials, would put the flag back on the ground where the artist had wanted it placed. In short, a work of art and protest interacted in a way that rarely happens, creating extraordinary daily performances. Even Congress interacted with these events, introducing in the Flag Protection Act, a few months later, a ban on laying the flag on the floor. Tyler, in turn, interacted with the act of Congress, participating in the flag burnings that led to its annulment by the Supreme Court in 1990. Tyler did these things together with members of the Revolutionary

Communist Party, whose ideas he shared. He also considered himself an anti-imperialist.[11]

The flags of Johns and other Pop artists (Oldenburg, Tom Wesselmann, William Copley), the works of Millett and Tyler and of Ringgold and Hammons found themselves together in the 1990s in the exhibition "Old Glory: The American Flag in Contemporary Art." They were not the only works present, but they formed the exhibit's leitmotif and represented its spirit. The curators said that they had trouble finding works that drew on the celebratory nineteenth-century tradition or simply the cheerful and bright tradition of a Hassam. Old Glory had, by then, become "politicized" in a critical or satirical sense, and there was nothing to be done. There was also a critical approach in the works of such photographers as Robert Frank, Diane Arbus, and Robert Mapplethorpe—with his magnificent "American Flag" (1977), torn and frayed, shot against the light. The exhibition opened in Cleveland in 1994 and had a relatively peaceful life. When, in 1996, it arrived in the Phoenix Art Museum in Arizona, it caused an uproar. Once again, as in Chicago in 1989, war veterans took the initiative in the protests from the first day. They picketed the museum, forced museum officials to close the doors in their face, to flee from a secondary entrance. As in Chicago, they passed to direct action, especially against the installations of Tyler and Millett. Again, they repeatedly and ritualistically removed the flags from the floor and the toilet, put them back "in order." The uproar assailed the city authorities. Some city council members asked that the exhibit be banned from the city. They threatened to dispose of the museum, which is municipal property, to sell it. The mayor, however, did nothing. A state legislator called for investigating the curators for breach of the state's flag-desecration law, although similar laws elsewhere had been struck down as unconstitutional way back in 1989.[12] And so, despite everything, the exhibition was not interrupted.

Of course, in all these years the flag has appeared in other cultural products, in more occasions and more contexts than I can count.[13] I do not, therefore, put forward any conclusions in this regard. I merely recall

Dread Scott, *What Is the Proper Way to Display a U.S. Flag?* (1989). (Courtesy Dread Scott)

how easy it is to mention film and pop-rock musical events in which the national emblem has been used in an ironic or problematic or, in any case, noncelebratory manner. There is the flag in the opening scene of the film *Patton* (1970) or in *Born on the Fourth of July* (1989) or in the whole of *Flags of Our Fathers* (2006), on Peter Fonda's jacket and motorcycle as "Captain America" in *Easy Rider* (1969), or on the diaper with which Woody Harrelson appears in court in *The People vs. Larry Flynt* (1996). There is the involuntary, comical desecration of the Stars-and-Stripes pants wearing which Sylvester Stallone tackles Soviet prizefighter Ivan "I must break you" Drago, in *Rocky IV* (1985). There is the cover of the album *Born in the USA* (1984), in which Bruce Springsteen seems to question the flag about the true meaning of America, its original values, the fate of the working-class hero to whom he loves to give voice. And there is the alluring Stars and Stripes that envelopes Madonna, in a red bikini and black boots, in an MTV commercial in 1990; she invites young people to vote, while she raps,

> Dr. King, Malcolm X
> Freedom of Speech
> Is as Good as Sex.
> And If You Do not Vote
> You're Going to Get a Spankie.

And there is *America: A Tribute to Heroes* (2001), the compact disc that honors the victims of September 11 with a set of songs that is as ambivalent and blasé as the *Flag, 1954–55* of Johns that dominates the cover: it opens with Springsteen's sad "My City of Ruin," it includes John Lennon's "Imagine" (sung by Neil Young), and it ends with "God Bless America" (Celine Dion) and "America the Beautiful" (Willie Nelson). Regarding Willie Nelson, and in many ways despite him, if there is an environment that has unreservedly kept intact a cult of the flag, a little schmaltzy and aggressive, it is that of country music—white and Southern by origins, and for at least forty years the favorite music of conservative patriots throughout the country.[14]

14 Capture the Flag

After September 11, flags once again invaded the United States. Stocks held by domestic producers ran out after a few hours, and retailers were forced to commit the ultimate impiety of marketing flags made abroad (the nation's totem should at least be Made in the USA). The most famous flag is the one hoisted by three firefighters at Ground Zero, on the ruins of the World Trade Center, recorded in the photograph-symbol of one of the most photographed events at the turn of the millennium.[1] That image evokes others, in the memory of Americans and in mine. It evokes, because of its plastic composition and pathos, and the declared intention of photographer Tom Franklin, who shot it, the Iwo Jima marines. It evokes the spectral ruins of Atlanta and Richmond in the pictures of the Civil War, the last time Americans really experienced war in their own land and the first time modern warfare, with its destructive fury toward civilian things and populations, unleashed its full power. It evokes, finally, filtered through the memory of so many film inventions, the drama of farms and forts and pioneer wagons attacked and laid waste by Indians in the near or far West. The shock of rediscovering the devastating effects of mass violence at home, just like the spirit of Iwo Jima and the spirit of the West, contributed to shaping the first popular reactions and those of the government authorities. For a moment, the Stars and Stripes was a flag of pain, mourning, and solidarity and therefore everyone's flag, including those who until then had felt no special patriotic passions. And thus it remained for many Americans. Almost immediately, however, it also once again acquired its multiplicity of meanings. Groups and individuals sought to carry it with them along different paths, to snatch it from one another. Once again, the national totem became an object of contention in a very serious game of capture the flag.

From here to there Stars and Stripes at Ground Zero, September 11, 2001. (AP Photo/ Beth A. Keiser)

The contention was, literally, and in many ways, about the Ground Zero flag itself. The famous picture should have been the basis of a bronze statue to be placed at the Brooklyn headquarters of the New York Fire Department, as a memorial to the firefighters—the most courageous and gentle of public servants, working-class civic heroes par excellence, honored by an ecumenical totem-flag that embraces and protects the whole community. But nothing is so simple in a complex, multiethnic, multiracial, stratified society. The three men photographed were white. When the plan for the statue was unveiled, the men had been changed to white, black, and Latino, in order to include, symbolically, all those who had perished in the Twin Towers (of the 343 firefighters killed at the World Trade Center, two dozen were not white). The attempted symbolic inclusion, however, backfired on the proposers. The white firefighters protested at the "politically correct" manipulation of reality by authorities and artists.[2] The black and Latino firefighters, instead, called for a real inclusion, as the New York Fire Department is 95 percent white, the least integrated of the largest cities. Perhaps this episode underlines a general feature of the post–September 11 flag patriotism, namely, that it affected most the white, ethnic working class and lower middle class, while racial minorities such as African Americans were less touched,[3] and affluent whites were less emotionally involved. It was in the white popular neighborhoods that the Stars and Stripes sprang up more numerously and had more warmth: often small and printed (not sewn), made of plastic or paper, hung on trees, taped to windows and mailboxes, displayed on cars and T-shirts as if they were the logo of a favorite team or rock band (not the proper way to treat Old Glory). All these were painful rites, and sometimes frustrating ones; some citizens said that they had flown the flag because they did not know what else to do: it was the only way to feel part of the community.[4] In white, affluent neighborhoods, on the other hand, the flags were large, sewn, made of good bunting; they were also cold, displayed in front yards as dictated by the Flag Code, and left there.

In October 2001, the Ground Zero flag passed from the hands of the firemen to those of the political and military authorities, and it celebrated other rites. Signed by the mayor of New York City, Rudolph Giuliani, and the New York governor, George Pataki, it was taken on board the carrier USS *Theodore Roosevelt* en route to Afghanistan and operation Enduring Freedom; or so everyone thought until it was discovered that it was not the original flag, that the original had disappeared (and is still being looked for).[5] Whether genuine or false, that flag became a symbol of retaliation and war; the blood of the incognizant martyrs with which it was soaked served to sanctify the renewed pride of the nation-state and its vocation to expand itself and its idea of freedom. The Stars and Stripes reappeared in this role in the spring of 2003, in the operation Iraqi Freedom, albeit with some embarrassment or shame. One was hoisted by the Marines in Umm Qasar, an Iraqi city just beyond the Kuwaiti border, in the first days of the war. But it was immediately lowered in accordance with superior orders; it could send, it was said, the wrong message, a message of conquest rather than liberation.[6] Another Stars and Stripes came out in the last days of the war, in the wrong place and time, in Baghdad, draped over the face of a twenty-foot statue of Saddam Hussein before it was pulled down. The scene lasted a few seconds, the result of the rash patriotic enthusiasm of Marine Corporal Edward Chin (a son of immigrants from Burma, the pride of his family and his neighborhood, Bensonhurst in Brooklyn). Once again the flag was hurriedly removed: these were not the orders, it was not meant to end like this.[7] But nevertheless a photograph captured the instant, and it would have remained the most striking image of that adventure—if it had not been eclipsed by subsequent and more vivid images of an adventure gone sour: the mass carnage in the streets of Iraq, the rows of coffins draped in the Stars and Stripes waiting to come back to the United States, the bodies of the tortured and the torturers in the Abu Ghraib Prison.[8]

There was no embarrassment or shame at all, on the contrary, among the conservative intellectuals who extolled the empire, who referred to it without any false modesty, and whom the writer Norman Mailer has called "the flag conservatives."[9] They believed, like other Americans before them, that the Stars and Stripes was not only suited to govern the world but that it should do so, that national security and the advancement of the cause of freedom were the same thing. There was here an impetus of revolutionary origin in which universalism, provincialism, and hard expansionism were intertwined: the idea that the American flag is a message of freedom for all; that everyone, after all, wants to be American; and that, if necessary, these repressed desires can be satisfied by an exported revolution from above. There was, as Randolph Bourne said in the days of Woodrow Wilson about Wilsonism, a "revival of our primitive Yankee boastfulness, the reversion of senility to that republican childhood when we expected the whole world to copy our republican institutions."[10] There was, I would add, the regression to a petulant Frontier adolescence, when the Yankee invaders thought they were the purveyors

From here to there The Stars and Stripes in Baghdad, April 9, 2003. Corporal Edward Chin, from New York, of the 3rd Battalion, 4th Marines regiment, places a U.S. flag on the face of Iraqi President Saddam Hussein's statue before tearing it down in downtown Baghdad. (AP Photo/Laurent Rebours)

of civilization in the land of others, in an open space without boundaries, except that, with a fatal overturning of logic and history, they felt unfairly threatened by "savages" (meaning the locals) inside the sacred confines of their own (newly intruded) homes. If the threat becomes a real attack, it is thought to be the result of evil, without a real reason.[11] And in fact the flag conservatives incredulously asked, "Why do they hate us?" in a dramatic and grotesque crescendo; they included among the America haters those Americans (the Left, the liberals) who were seeking plausible answers to this question.[12] America was for them pure elegy, *A Heart, a Cross, and a Flag*.[13]

The imperial flag was greeted by the active consensus of part of the population. There were demonstrations of support for the government and "our troops" in many cities, on the part of community and patriotic groups, Harley-Davidson bikers, others. Country music, with a little help from southern rock, provided a soundtrack of new hymns to the old Red, White, and Blue.[14] On various occasions, in the streets of the country, the Stars and Stripes changed from being an emblem of civic union to an emblem of hostility toward the enemies, the distant ones and the near—the Arab or Muslim immigrants and the political dissidents. There were occasions when cars decorated with flags sometimes improvised lengthy columns, with aggressive bumper stickers ("You are either with us or against us," to quote President George W. Bush) and with an intimidatory attitude toward those who had no flag; and the most decorated cars were the most macho, SUVs and pickups.[15] But it was precisely this "sectarian" appropriation of the national totem that created some problems for its appeal. During the Iraqi campaign, sales of flags remained stable; the boom of 2001 was not repeated, partly because the market was saturated, partly because the public was divided and uncertain. Even businesses displayed caution in the exploitation of the national colors for marketing purposes, after the intoxication of the previous months—for fear, now, of being misunderstood. An advertising agent said, "people have different feelings about the war; any patriotic advertising could be construed as supporting the war rather than supporting America as a whole as after September

11."[16] There was, in other words, the risk of alienating sizeable groups of consumers, and citizens.

This risk soon became apparent because, in fact, civic solidarity, freedom, and war can be incompatible; they can be at odds. In fact, as always in times of national emergency, in the name of the flag and patriotic unity, there was a crescendo of accusations of disloyalty against whoever exercised the freedom to dissent. And the federal government adopted measures that, starting with the so-called USA Patriot Act (which came into force on October 26, 2001, and had been discussed in the preceding weeks), limited the civil rights of certain categories of people. The reactions to these developments can be summarized through a series of satirical cartoons that appeared within a few days in the *Washington Post*, signed by the same artist, Pat Oliphant. The first cartoon, of September 13, shows the immediate reaction: a furious Uncle Sam, dressed in Stars and Stripes, rolls up his sleeves and advances menacingly toward the reader and the enemy. In the second cartoon, of September 17, the flag-clad Uncle Sam is armed with a sword and ready to strike blindly around him, but behind him, close to the blade of the sword and in obvious danger, there is a child with a small Stars and Stripes in his hands and the words "civil liberties" inscribed on his T-shirt. "Watch out for the backswing, kid," Uncle Sam warns him. On whose side, therefore, are the national colors? Are there perhaps two flags, that of empire and that of freedom, potentially clashing? The third cartoon, of October 4, is a narrative strip. The office boss tells the employee that, because of the country's great tragedy, owing to circumstances beyond his control, he is forced to fire him. "Being the staunch patriot you are," he says, "we knew you would understand. Goodbye and good luck." He adds, "Have a flag," handing it to him. Here the flag becomes, just as can happen with patriotism, an instrument for settling internal scores and the last refuge of the scoundrel.

The flag conservatives, who are Republicans, equated flag, country, government, and presidential administration and viewed criticism of government policies—their policies—as unpatriotic. Their assault on the

Here The flag and civil liberties, September 17, 2001. (Cartoon by Oliphant, Copyright 2001 Universal Press Syndicate; reprinted with permission; all rights reserved.).

previous administration, the Democratic administration of Bill Clinton, was part of the fight against the "haters" of America and was therefore legitimate. The Democrats suffered this strange logic with timidity. Having decided since the days of Ronald Reagan, triumphant not to let anyone outflag them, they devoted themselves to a subordinate and slightly pathetic flag-waving, not disputing the meaning that the conservatives gave to patriotism and the flag and lining up behind the decisions of the Bush administration. Those who gave the Stars and Stripes a different meaning were radical and left-liberal groups who grew into an opposition movement. Initially there was some resistance to the use of the flag, due to old political grudges, historical amnesia, frivolous anxieties, what the sociologist and polemicist Todd Gitlin has called "our sixties flag anxiety." Wasn't the flag an icon of the Right, an icon of warmongering nationalism? Isn't it a therapeutic amulet giving false security and a feeling of innocence?

Isn't it a little kitsch? But, on the other hand, how can one ignore its popular diffusion? After September 11, noted novelist Erica Jong, even drag queens wear flag dresses (actually they have always done so).[17] Gradually, there was the (re)discovery that the national flag could embody ideas that the Left shares and for which it has fought, and that its repudiation hindered their dialogue with their fellow citizens. Writer Barbara Kingsolver has told the story of her conversion, from refusal to doubt ("any symbol conceived in liberty deserves the benefit of the doubt") and then to the determination not to leave that symbol to others. *Their* flag represents intimidation, violence, and contempt for the Constitution? "Well, *our* flag does not, and I'm determined that it never will."[18]

To reclaim the national flag, to challenge the conservatives' monopoly of patriotic language, was the attempt of a part of the antiwar movement

Patriots Antiwar rally, Washington, D.C., April 10, 2004. Protestors march toward the White House during a rally against the war in Iraq, a year after the U.S. capture of Baghdad. (AP Photo/Manuel Balce Ceneta)

Patriots Prowar rally, Washington, D.C., March 17, 2007. March on the Pentagon Anti-War Rally and Vietnam Vet/Iraq Vet Pro-War Counter Rally on the four-year anniversary of the Iraq War. (Photo by Daniel Hammontree)

in the months that preceded and accompanied the invasion of Iraq. This effort produced another "sectarian" totem-flag, this time a pacifist one. The Stars and Stripes is the flag of freedom of speech, and it belongs to the country and not the government, much less to this liberticidal administration, said old liberals such as Arthur Schlesinger, Jr., and Bill Moyers; Moyers paraphrased Thoreau: "standing up to your government can mean standing up for your country."[19] Even as caustic a radical as Gore Vidal appeared on the flag-decked cover of the leftist weekly the *Nation*, with a cover story entitled "We Are the Patriots."[20] Other progressives squabbled over the merits of a "patriotic left" that would leave the isolation of groupuscule politics or the academic intellectuals (concerned with conquering the English or history departments, while the Right was conquering the White House) and seek, in the name of "American ideals," to mobilize citizens and turn on the opponents the accusations of antipatriotism. Whoever denies the rights of defense to those accused of terrorism, whoever lies about the reasons for a war, whoever is friend to corporate leaders who cook the books, whoever condones poverty and social inequalities—here is who disgraces the flag. Against wars that one does not agree with, it is right to bring into the streets Stars and Stripes announcing that "peace is patriotic."[21] Quite a few such flags were carried by protesters at the antiwar rallies of 2003. Not all the participants liked what they saw. There were verbal clashes with other protesters who

Patriots Large and small flags of mourning, New York, September 11, 2002. On the one-year anniversary of the 9/11 terrorist attack on the World Trade Center, a woman places a small Puerto Rican flag next to a large Stars and Stripes in a circle of remembrances left by family members and friends of victims at Ground Zero. (AP Photo/Mike Segar, Pool)

considered themselves anti-imperialist and internationalist and considered the national flag a symbol of imperialism. And there were other Stars and Stripes, carried upside down (in the tradition of the Vietnam era), with stripes dripping blood (in the style of Faith Ringgold), with the stars replaced by skulls (in the style of Mark Twain) or by the trademarks of giant corporations.[22] Who owns the Stars and Stripes? The game could not but go on. And it is still going on.

Notes

NOTES TO THE INTRODUCTION

1. Carolyn Marvin and David W. Ingle, *Blood Sacrifice and the Nation: Totem Rituals and the American Flag* (New York: Cambridge University Press, 1999); Michael Billig, *Banal Nationalism* (London: Sage, 1995), 39. The "cult of the flag" quotation is from French philosopher Ernest Renan's 1882 lecture, "Qu'est-ce qu'une nation?" translated "What Is a Nation?" in *Nation and Narration*, ed. Homi K. Bhabha (New York: Routledge, 1990), 17.

2. Jeffrey Fleishman, "Rage over Cartoons Perplexes Denmark," *Los Angeles Times*, February 9, 2006; Stacy Meichtry, "Denmark's Flag, Now Burned by Muslims, Has Christian Past," *National Catholic Reporter*, February 24, 2006.

3. See the papers presented at the conference "Flying the Flag: Critical Perspectives on Symbolism and Identity," University of Oslo, November 24–25, 2005, available online at http://www.culcom.uio.no/aktivitet/flagg-konferanse/abstracts.html (accessed December 23, 2007); Nick Groom, *The Union Jack: The Biography* (London: Atlantic, 2006).

4. "Flag Burning, National Symbols and Free Speech: Issues, Regulations, Studies," *Caslon Analytics*, http://www.caslon.com.au/flagfiresnote.htm (accessed December 21, 2007).

5. Raoul Girardet, "Les trois couleurs," in *Les lieux de mémoire*, ed. Pierre Nora (Paris: Gallimard, 1984), 1:5–37; Maurice Dommanget, *Histoire du drapeau rouge: Des origines à la guerre de 1939* (Paris: Editions Libraire de l'Etoile, 1966); Ersilia Alessandrone Perona, "La bandiera rossa," in *I luoghi della memoria*, ed. Mario Isnenghi (Rome-Bari: Laterza, 1997), 293–316.

6. Michael Kammen, *Mystic Chords of Memory: The Transformation of Tradition in American Culture* (New York: Vintage, 1993), 294; Raffaella Baritono, "Uno stato a 'bassa intensità'? L'esperienza storica statunitense," *Scienza e Politica* 32 (2005): 25–53.

7. George Mosse, *The Nationalization of the Masses: Political Symbolism and Mass Movements in Germany* (New York: H. Fertig, 1975); Maurice Agulhon, *Marianne into Battle: Republican Imagery and Symbolism in France, 1789–1880* (New York: Cambridge University Press, 1981); Maurice Agulhon, *Marianne au pouvoir: L'imagerie et la symbolique républicaines de 1880 à 1914* (Paris: Flammarion, 1989);

Maurizio Ridolfi, *Le feste nazionali* (Bologna: Il Mulino, 2003); Gianni Oliva, "Il tricolore," in Isnenghi, *I luoghi della memoria*, 3–32; *Gli italiani e il Tricolore: Patriottismo, identità nazionale e fratture sociali lungo due secoli di storia*, ed. Fiorenza Tarozzi and Giorgio Vecchio (Bologna: Il Mulino, 1999); Alistair B. Fraser, "The Flags of Canada," website of Alistair B. Fraser, 1998, http://fraser.cc/FlagsCan/ (accessed December 21, 2007); Enrique Florescano, *La bandera mexicana: Breve historia de su formación y simbolismo* (Mexico City: Fondo de Cultura Economica, 1998); Fleurimond W. Kerns, "The Birth of the Haitian Flag," in *Haiti: A Slave Revolution*, ed. Pat Chin (New York: International Action Center, 2004), 99–115; Carol A. Foley, *The Australian Flag: Colonial Relic or Contemporary Icon?* (Leichhardt, NSW: Federation, 1996); John W. Dower, *War without Mercy: Race and Power in the Pacific War* (New York: Pantheon, 1986); Arundhati Virmani, "National Symbols under Colonial Domination: The Nationalization of the Indian Flag, March–August 1923," *Past and Present* 164 (August 1999): 169–97.

8. Edmund Wilson, *Patriotic Gore: Studies in the Literature of the American Civil War* (New York: Oxford University Press, 1962), xii–xiii. Even small Haiti, whose flag is claimed to carry a universal message of freedom for the "African race," a few years after completing its revolution conquered Spanish Santo Domingo and ruled it until it finally attained independence as the Dominican Republic in 1844.

9. Thomas Paine, *Common Sense* (1776; New York: Penguin, 1986), 120, 63.

10. Walt Whitman, *Democratic Vistas* (1871), in *The Portable Walt Whitman*, ed. Mark Van Doren, rev. ed. Malcolm Cowley (New York: Penguin, 1977), 369.

11. Eric Foner, *The Story of American Freedom* (New York: Norton, 1998).

12. Marvin and Ingle, *Blood Sacrifice and the Nation*; Alberto Mario Banti, *L'onore della nazione: Identità sessuali e violenza nel nazionalismo europeo dal XVIII secolo alla Grande Guerra* (Turin: Einaudi, 2005).

13. Drew Gilpin Faust, *"This Republic of Suffering": Death and the American Civil War* (New York: Knopf, 2008).

14. Walt Whitman, "Song of the Banner at Daybreak," in *Drum-Taps* (1865), in *Leaves of Grass*, ed. Jerome Loving (1891; New York: Oxford University Press, 1990), 228.

15. Thomas Jefferson to William S. Smith, Paris, November 13, 1787, in Thomas Jefferson, *Writings*, ed. Merrill D. Peterson (New York: Library of America, 1984), 911; John Brown quotation from the New Testament (Hebrews 9:22) in James M. McPherson, *Battle Cry of Freedom: The Civil War Era* (New York: Oxford University Press, 1988), 203.

16. Frederick Douglass, "There Was a Right Side in the Late War," speech delivered at Union Square, New York City, on Decoration Day, May 30, 1878, in

Frederick Douglass: Selected Speeches and Writings, ed. Philip S. Foner, abridged and adapted by Yuval Taylor (Chicago: Lawrence Hill Books, 1999), 627, 631.

17. "Somebody Paid the Price for Your Right: Register/Vote," poster, A. Philip Randolph Educational Fund, ca. 1968, Gary Yanker Collection, Prints and Photographs Division, Library of Congress.

18. Mark Twain, *Roughing It* (1871; New York: Penguin, 1981), 405–6.

19. Henri-Félix-Emmanuel Philippoteaux (1815–1884), *Lamartine devant l'Hôtel de Ville de Paris, le 25 février 1848* (1848), Musée Carnavalet, Paris; Lamartine's quotation in John S. C. Abbot, *The History of Napoleon III, Emperor of France* (1868; Ann Arbor: Scholarly Publishing Office, University of Michigan Library, 2005), 313.

20. Arnaldo Testi, "Again, Why Is There No Socialism in the United States?" *Storia Nordamericana* 7:1 (1990): 59–92; the reference is to Werner Sombart, *Warum gibt es in den Vereinigten Staaten keinen Sozialismus?* (1906) translated as *Why Is There No Socialism in the United States?* (Armonk, N.Y.: M. E. Sharpe, 1978).

NOTES TO CHAPTER 1

1. Michael Kammen, *A Season of Youth: The American Revolution and the Historical Imagination* (New York: Knopf, 1978), 28–29.

2. The main texts on the history of the flag that I have used throughout the book are Scot M. Guenter, *The American Flag, 1777–1924: Cultural Shifts from Creation to Codification* (Cranbury, N.J.: Associated University Presses, 1990); Marc Leepson, *Flag: An American Biography* (New York: St. Martin's, 2005); and George Henry Preble, *Origin and History of the American Flag*, new ed., with a supplement by Charles Edward Asnis, 2 vols. (Philadelphia: N. L. Brown, 1917)—a fine, patriotic nineteenth-century contribution. For their lavish pictorials, I perused and enjoyed William Rea Furlong and Byron McCandless, *So Proudly We Hail: The History of the United States Flag* (Washington, D.C.: Smithsonian Institution Press, 1981); Boleslaw Mastai and Marie-Louise D'Otrange Mastai, *The Stars and the Stripes: The American Flag as Art and as History from the Birth of the Republic to the Present* (Old Saybrook, Conn.: Konecky & Konecky, 1973); and Deborah Harding, *Stars and Stripes: Patriotic Motifs in American Folk Art* (New York: Rizzoli, 2002).

3. Lester C. Olson, *Emblems of American Community in the Revolutionary Era: A Study in Rhetorical Iconology* (Washington, D.C.: Smithsonian Institution Press, 1991), 21–74.

4. Loretta Valtz Mannucci, "Aquile e tacchini: Iconografie di stato," in *L'estetica della politica*, ed. Maurizio Vaudagna (Rome-Bari: Laterza, 1989), 151–71.

5. Washington Irving, "Rip Van Winkle," in *The Sketch Book of Geoffrey Crayon, Gent.* (1819; New York: New American Library, 1981), 48–49, 53.

6. William J. Canby, "The History of the Flag of the United States" (1870), a paper read before the Historical Society of Pennsylvania, available online at http://www.ushistory.org/betsy/more/canby.htm (accessed January 10, 2008). Three of Betsy Ross's surviving female relatives supported Canby's statements at the time. See their affidavits: Sophia B. Hildebrant (Betsy's granddaughter), Philadelphia, May 27, 1870; Margaret Donaldson Boggs (Betsy's niece), Philadelphia, June 3, 1870; and Rachel Fletcher (Betsy's daughter), New York City, July 31, 1871; all available online at http://www.ushistory.org/betsy/flagaffs.html (accessed January 10, 2008).

7. JoAnn Menezes, "The Birthing of the American Flag and the Invention of an American Founding Mother in the Image of Betsy Ross," in *Narratives of Nostalgia, Gender, and Nationalism*, ed. Jean Pickering and Suzanne Kehde (New York: New York University Press, 1997), 74–87.

8. Amy Swerdlow, "The Congress of American Women: Left-Feminist Peace Politics in the Cold War," in *U.S. History as Women's History: New Feminist Essays*, ed. Linda K. Kerber, Alice Kessler-Harris, and Kathryn Kish Sklar (Chapel Hill: University of North Carolina Press, 1995), 306.

9. Michael Frisch, "American History and the Structures of Collective Memory: A Modest Exercise in Empirical Iconography," *Journal of American History* 75 (March 1989): 1130–55.

NOTES TO CHAPTER 2

1. Michael Kimmel, *Manhood in America: A Cultural History* (New York: Free Press, 1996), 36–38; Joel H. Silbey, *The American Political Nation, 1838–1893* (Palo Alto, Calif.: Stanford University Press, 1991), 69–71, 86–90.

2. John M. Coski, *The Confederate Battle Flag: America's Most Embattled Emblem* (Cambridge, Mass.: Harvard University Press, 2005); Robert E. Bonner, *Colors and Blood: Flag Passions of the Confederate South* (Princeton, N.J.: Princeton University Press, 2002).

3. Raimondo Luraghi, *Storia della guerra civile americana* (Turin: Einuadi, 1966), 1270.

4. Cecilia Elizabeth O'Leary, *To Die For: The Paradox of American Patriotism* (Princeton, N.J.: Princeton University Press, 1999); Matthew Dennis, *Red, White, and Blue Letter Days: An American Calendar* (Ithaca, N.Y.: Cornell University Press, 2002); Ellen M. Litwicki, *America's Public Holidays, 1865–1920* (Washington, D.C.: Smithsonian Institution Press, 2000); Stuart McConnell, "Reading the Flag: A

Reconsideration of the Patriotic Cults of the 1890s," in *Bonds of Affection: Americans Define Their Patriotism*, ed. John Bodnar (Princeton, N.J.: Princeton University Press, 1996), 102–19; David Glassberg, *American Historical Pageantry: The Uses of Tradition in the Early Twentieth Century* (Chapel Hill: University of North Carolina Press, 1990); Karal Ann Marling, *George Washington Slept Here: Colonial Revivals and American Culture, 1876–1986* (Cambridge, Mass.: Harvard University Press, 1988).

5. David Waldstreicher, *In the Midst of Perpetual Fetes: The Making of American Nationalism, 1776–1820* (Chapel Hill: University of North Carolina Press, 1997); Len Travers, *Celebrating the Fourth: Independence Day and the Rites of Nationalism in the Early Republic* (Amherst: University of Massachusetts Press, 1997).

6. William L. Riordon, *Plunkitt of Tammany Hall*, ed. Terence J. McDonald (1905; New York: St. Martin's, 1994), 86–88.

7. David D. Blight, *Race and Reunion: The Civil War in American Memory* (Cambridge, Mass.: Harvard University Press, 2001).

8. Nina Silber, *The Romance of Reunion: Northerners and the South, 1865–1900* (Chapel Hill: University of North Carolina Press, 1993), 58–60.

9. Stuart McConnell, *Glorious Contentment: The Grand Army of the Republic, 1865–1900* (Chapel Hill: University of North Carolina Press, 1992); Wallace E. Davies, *Patriotism on Parade: The Story of Veterans' and Hereditary Organizations in America, 1783–1900* (Cambridge, Mass.: Harvard University Press, 1955).

10. Louis Kaplan, "A Patriotic Mole: A Living Photograph," *CR: The New Centennial Review* 1 (Spring 2001): 107–39.

11. Percy MacKay, "Washington and Betsy Ross: A Dramatic Action in Two Scenes," in *Plays for Patriotic Days*, ed. Robert Haven Schauffler and A. P. Sanford (New York: Dodd, Mead, 1928), 95. This piece is the abridged version of a longer historical pageant: Percy MacKay, *Washington: The Man Who Made Us* (New York: Knopf, 1919).

12. Quoted in Richard J. Ellis, *To the Flag: The Unlikely History of the Pledge of Allegiance* (Lawrence: University Press of Kansas, 2005), 123, 28–29.

13. Leigh Eric Schmidt, *Consumer Rites: The Buying and Selling of American Holidays* (Princeton, N.J.: Princeton University Press, 1995).

NOTES TO CHAPTER 3

1. Randolph S. Bourne, "The State" (1918), in *War and the Intellectuals: Collected Essays, 1915–1919*, ed. Carl Resek (New York: Harper & Row, 1964), 71, 74, 87.

2. George Creel, *How We Advertised America: The First Telling of the Amazing*

Story of the Committee on Public Information That Carried the Gospel of Americanism to Every Corner of the Globe (New York: Macmillan, 1920), 3–9.

3. Ellen Carol DuBois and Lynn Dumenil, *Through Women's Eyes: An American History with Documents* (Boston: Bedford/St. Martin's, 2005), 454–59.

4. "The Government Presents," *New York Times*, May 26, 1918. See also "Pershing Film Gives Vast View of War," *New York Times*, May 22, 1918; "Film Our Men in Trenches: Second Feature of 'Following the Flag to France' Is Ready," *New York Times*, July 15, 1918; "Official Film Tells How War Was Won: 'Under Four Flags' Shows Pershing's Crusaders in Last Word of America's Answer," *New York Times*, November 18, 1918.

5. Quoted in Rogan Kersh, *Dreams of a More Perfect Union* (Ithaca, N.Y.: Cornell University Press, 2001), 276.

6. Quoted in Marvin and Ingle, *Blood Sacrifice and the Nation*, 39.

7. The present text of the federal Flag Code is in *U.S. Code,* title 4, chapter 1.

8. Kurt Vonnegut, Jr., *Breakfast of Champions* (London: Granada, 1974), 18.

9. Mark Dyreson, "'This Flag Dips for No Earthly King': The Mysterious Origins of an American Myth," *International Journal of the History of Sport* 25 (February 2008): 142–62; Mark Dyreson, "'To Dip or Not to Dip': The American Flag at the Olympic Games Since 1936," *International Journal of the History of Sport* 25 (February 2008): 163–84.

10. Quotations from *Michael A. Newdow v. U.S. Congress et al.*, U.S. Court of Appeals for the Ninth Circuit, 292 F.3d 597 (2002). On these events, see Ellis, *To the Flag*, 125–42.

11. Quotations from *Newdow v. U.S. Congress* and from Barry A. Kismin and Seymour P. Lachman, *One Nation under God: Religion in Contemporary America* (New York: Crown, 1993), 25.

12. Willard B. Gatewood, "Theodore Roosevelt and the Coinage Controversy," *American Quarterly* 18 (Spring 1966): 35–51.

NOTES TO CHAPTER 4

1. John E. Semonche, *Keeping the Faith: A Cultural History of the U.S. Supreme Court* (Lanham, Md.: Rowman & Littlefield, 1998); James Bryce, *The American Commonwealth,* 3rd rev. ed. (New York: Macmillan, 1893), 1:266.

2. *Minersville School District v. Gobitis*, 310 U.S. 586 (1940). On the entire controversy, see *The Constitution and the Flag*, vol. 1, *The Flag Salute Cases*, ed. Michael K. Curtis (New York: Garland, 1993).

3. *West Virginia Board of Education v. Barnette*, 319 U.S. 624 (1943).

4. John Bodnar, *Remaking America: Public Memory, Commemoration, and Patriotism in the Twentieth Century* (Princeton, N.J.: Princeton University Press, 1992), 237.

5. *Michael A. Newdow v. U.S. Congress et al.*, U.S. Court of Appeals for the Ninth Circuit, 292 F.3d 597 (2002).

6. Karen DeYoung, "Bush: Pledge Ruling Reinforced Need for 'Common Sense' Judges," *Washington Post*, June 27, 2002; *An Act to Reaffirm the Reference to One Nation under God in the Pledge of Allegiance*, 107th Congress, 2d Session, S. 2690 (2002); David Montgomery, "Rise! Shine! Give 'Under God' Your Glory!" *Washington Post*, June 28, 2002.

7. Judge Stephen Reinhardt quoted in Charles Lane, "Pledge of Allegiance Ruling Is Upheld," *Washington Post*, March 1, 2003.

8. *Elk Grove Unified School District et al. v. Michael A. Newdow et al.*, 542 U.S. 1 (2004); Ellis, *To the Flag*, 142–52.

NOTES TO CHAPTER 5

1. Yvonne Korshak, "The Liberty Cap as a Revolutionary Symbol in America and France," *Smithsonian Studies in American Art* 1 (Autumn 1987): 52–69.

2. Irvin Molotsky, *The Flag, the Poet and the Song: The Story of the Star-Spangled Banner* (New York: Dutton, 2001); Lonn Taylor, *The Star-Spangled Banner: The Flag That Inspired the National Anthem* (New York: Harry N. Abrams, National Museum of American History, and Smithsonian Institution, 2000).

3. Mark E. Needy, Jr., and Harold Holzer, *The Union Image: Popular Prints of the Civil War North* (Chapel Hill: University of North Carolina Press, 2000).

4. Quoted in McPherson, *Battle Cry of Freedom*, vi.

5. Michael Corcoran, *For Which It Stands: An Anecdotal Biography of the American Flag* (New York: Simon & Schuster, 2002), 97, 92.

6. Abraham Lincoln, "Speech at Independence Hall, Philadelphia, Pennsylvania," February 22, 1861, in *Selected Speeches and Writings by Abraham Lincoln*, introd. Gore Vidal (New York: Library of America, 1992), 282–83; William Lloyd Garrison, *The Spirit of the South towards Northern Freemen and Soldiers Defending the American Flag against Traitors of the Deepest Dye* (Boston: R. F. Wallcut, 1861); Frederick Douglass, *Life and Times of Frederick Douglass, Written by Himself* (Hartford, Conn.: Park, 1881), 348.

7. Quoted in *The Rebellion Record: A Diary of American Events*, ed. Frank Moore (New York: G. P. Putnam, 1862), 3:35.

8. Eric Foner, *Nothing but Freedom: Emancipation and Its Legacy* (Baton Rouge: Louisiana State University Press, 1983).

9. Tiziano Bonazzi, *La Dichiarazione di Indipendenza degli Stati Uniti d'America* (Venice: Marsilio, 2003); Robert A. Dahl, *How Democratic Is the American Constitution?* (New Haven, Conn.: Yale University Press, 2001).

10. Frederick Douglass, "The Meaning of July Fourth for the Negro," speech at Rochester, New York, July 5, 1852, in *Frederick Douglass: Selected Speeches and Writings*, 188–205.

11. Quoted in Franny Nudelman, *John Brown's Body: Slavery, Violence, and the Culture of War* (Chapel Hill: University of North Carolina Press, 2004), 135.

12. Douglass, *Life and Times of Frederick Douglass*, 418.

13. Merle Curti, *The Roots of American Loyalty* (New York: Columbia University Press, 1946); Robert H. Wiebe, *Who We Are: A History of Popular Nationalism* (Princeton, N.J.: Princeton University Press, 2002).

NOTES TO CHAPTER 6

1. Werner Sollors, *Beyond Ethnicity: Consent and Descent in American Culture* (New York: Oxford University Press, 1986).

2. The play's text is available online at http://www.gutenberg.org/etext/23893 (accessed January 10, 2008).

3. John Higham, *Strangers in the Land: Patterns of American Nativism* (New Brunswick, N.J.: Rutgers University Press, 1955), 285–99; Wyn Craig Wade, *The Fiery Cross: The Ku Klux Klan in America* (New York: Simon & Schuster, 1987), 249–50.

4. Glen Jeansonne, *Gerald L. K. Smith, Minister of Hate* (New Haven, Conn.: Yale University Press, 1988).

5. Lucy G. Barber, *Marching on Washington: The Forging of an American Tradition* (Berkeley: University of California Press, 2002), 44–74; "Seneca Falls Declaration of Sentiments and Resolutions" (1848), in DuBois and Dumenil, *Through Women's Eyes*, A18–21.

6. Jacquelyn Dowd Hall, "Disorderly Women: Gender and Labor Militancy in the Appalachian South," *Journal of American History* 73:2 (September 1986): 373.

7. Michael Kazin and Steven J. Ross, "America's Labor Day: The Dilemma of a Workers' Celebration," *Journal of American History* 78 (March 1992): 1294–1323.

8. Jan Howard, "The Provocation of Violence: A Civil Rights Tactic," *Dissent* 13 (Spring 1966): 94–99; Warren Hinckle and David Welsh, "Five Battles of Selma: The South at War," *Ramparts* 4 (June 1965): 19–52; Taylor Branch, *Pillar of Fire: America in the King Years, 1963–1965* (New York: Simon & Schuster, 1998), 208–9;

Powerful Days: The Civil Rights Photography of Charles Moore, ed. Michael S. Durham (New York: Stewart, Tabori & Chang, 1991), 57, 200–201, 202, 204–5.

9. John Hillson, *The Battle of Boston* (New York: Pathfinder, 1977), 223–26; Ronald P. Formisano, *Boston against Busing* (Chapel Hill: University of North Carolina Press, 1991), 150; Louis P. Masur, *The Soiling of Old Glory: The Story of a Photograph That Shocked America* (New York: Bloomsbury, 2008).

NOTES TO CHAPTER 7

1. Sacvan Bercovitch, *The American Jeremiad* (Madison: University of Wisconsin Press, 1978); Michael Walzer, *Exodus and Revolution* (New York: Basic Books, 1985).

2. François Furet, *Interpreting the French Revolution*, trans. Elborg Forster (New York: Cambridge University Press, 1981), 10; Paolo Viola, "Napoléon, chef de la révolution patriotique," in *Napoléon et l'Europe: Colloque de la Roche-sur-Yon*, ed. Jean-Clément Martin (Rennes: Presses Universitaires, 2002), 33–44.

3. Earl Browder, *What Is Communism?* (New York: Vanguard, 1936), 19; Irving Howe and Lewis Coser, *The American Communist Party* (New York: Praeger, 1962), 339–41.

4. Langston Hughes, "The Negro Artist and the Racial Mountain," *Nation* 112 (June 1926): 692–94.

5. Langston Hughes, "Let America Be America Again" (1936), in *The Negro Caravan*, ed. Sterling A. Brown, Arthur P. Davis, and Ulysses Lee (New York: Dryden, 1941), 370–72.

6. Sacvan Bercovitch, *Rites of Assent: Transformations in the Symbolic Construction of America* (New York: Routledge, 1993), 87.

7. Langston Hughes, "Harlem," in *Montage of a Dream Deferred* (1951), in *Selected Poems* (New York: Vintage, 1959), 268.

8. John Wannuaucon Quinney, "Quinney's Speech" (July 4, 1854), in *The Heath Anthology of American Literature*, ed. Paul Lauter (Boston: Houghton Mifflin, 2002), 1:1405.

9. Malcolm X, "The Ballot or the Bullet" (1964), in *Malcolm X Speaks: Selected Speeches and Statements*, ed. George Breitman (New York: Grove, 1994), 23–44.

10. Judith Hole and Ellen Levine, *Rebirth of Feminism* (New York: Quadrangle/New York Times, 1971), 242.

NOTES TO CHAPTER 8

1. Walt Whitman, "More Stars for the Spangled Banner" (1846), in *The Gathering of the Forces*, ed. Cleveland Rodgers and John Black (New York: G. P. Putnam's Sons, 1920), 1:244–45.

2. [John O'Sullivan], "Annexation," in *U.S. Magazine and Democratic Review* 17 (July–August 1845): 5–10.

3. [Alexander Hamilton], "Federalist No. 6" (1787), in James Madison, Alexander Hamilton, and John Jay, *The Federalist Papers* (1788; New York: Penguin, 1987), 104–8.

4. Albert K. Weinberg, *Manifest Destiny: A Study of Nationalist Expansionism in American History* (Baltimore: Johns Hopkins University Press, 1935), 121–22.

5. The "Marines' Hymn," like other American hymns that originated in the nineteenth century, was set to music on a European theme, in this case taken from an opéra bouffe by the French composer Jacques Offenbach, *Geneviève de Brabant* (1867); it only became the official hymn of the Corps in 1929.

6. Anthony Trollope, *North America* (1862; New York: Penguin, 1992), 58.

7. Native Americans, especially Plains Indians, had a much more complex relationship with the Stars and Stripes. See Douglas A. Schmittou and Michael H. Logan, "Fluidity of Meaning: Flag Imagery in Plains Indian Art," *American Indian Quarterly* 26 (Fall 2002): 559–604.

8. Milo Milton Quaife, *The Flag of the United States* (New York: Grosset & Dunlap, 1942), 141–51; Willis F. Johnson, *The National Flag: A History* (Boston: Houghton Mifflin, 1930), 80.

9. Paul Andrew Hutton, "'Correct in Every Detail': General Custer in Hollywood," in *Legacy: New Perspectives on Little Bighorn*, ed. Charles E. Rankin (Helena: Montana Historical Society Press, 1996), 231–70; Brian W. Dippie, *Custer's Last Stand: The Anatomy of an American Myth* (Missoula: University of Montana Publications, 1976), 50–51.

10. Richard Slotkin, *Gunfighter Nation: The Myth of the Frontier in Twentieth-Century America* (New York: Atheneum, 1992), 76–82.

11. Susan Sontag, *Regarding the Pain of Others* (New York: Farrar, Straus and Giroux, 2003), 63–64.

12. Report to Admiral George Dewey, August 18, 1898, in Nathan Sargent, *Admiral Dewey and the Manila Campaign* (Washington, D.C.: Naval Historical Foundation, 1947), 111.

13. Albert J. Beveridge, "The March of the Flag" (1898), in *The Meaning of the Times and Other Speeches* (Indianapolis: Bobbs-Merrill, 1908), 49, 57.

14. William Jennings Bryan, "The National Emblem" (1898), in *Against the Beast: A Documentary History of American Opposition to Empire*, ed. John Nichols (New York: Nation Books, 2004), 110.

15. Mark Twain, "The American Flag" (1901) and "To the Person Sitting in Darkness" (1901), in *Mark Twain's Weapons of Satire: Anti-Imperialist Writings on the Philippine-American War*, ed. Jim Zwick (Syracuse, N.Y.: Syracuse University Press, 1992), 16–77, 37, 39.

16. Edgar Lee Masters, "Harry Wilmans," in *Spoon River Anthology* (New York: Macmillan, 1915), 186.

17. *Halter v. Nebraska*, 205 U.S. 34 (1907).

18. "L'espansione economica degli Stati Uniti all'estero," *Il Divenire Sociale*, December 31, 1909.

NOTES TO CHAPTER 9

1. Article 4, sec. 3, cl. 2 of the Constitution, the so-called Territorial Clause ("The Congress shall have power to dispose of and make all needful Rules and Regulations respecting the Territory or other Property belonging to the United States") seemed to give Congress the authority to govern the territories as it thought best. On the other hand, in 1857, the Supreme Court decided that "there is certainly no power given by the Constitution to the Federal Government to establish or maintain colonies bordering on the United States or at a distance, to be ruled and governed at its own pleasure, or to enlarge its territorial limits in any way, except by the admission of new states." *Dred Scott v. John F. A. Sandford*, 60 U.S. 393 (1857). This ruling is very well known because, in the inflamed climate preceding the Civil War, it laid down that slaves were private property and that no person of African origin could ever become a citizen of the United States.

2. Justice Henry B. Brown in *Samuel Downes v. George R. Bidwell*, 182 U.S. 244 (1901).

3. Joseph B. Foraker, "The United States and Puerto Rico," *North American Review* 170 (April 1900): 469.

4. See some of them in Donald Dewey, *The Art of Ill Will: The Story of American Political Cartoons* (New York: New York University Press, 2007), 39–45, 129–34.

5. George G. Vest, "Objections to Annexing the Philippines," *North American Review* 168 (January 1899): 112.

6. Democratic Party Platform of 1900, available online at http://www.presidency.ucsb.edu/ws/index.php?pid=29587 (accessed January 10, 2008).

7. Quoted in Bernard Schwartz, *A History of the Supreme Court* (New York: Oxford University Press, 1993), 173–74.

8. Article 1, sec. 8, cl. 1, the so-called Uniformity Clause.

9. Quoted in *Samuel Downes v. George R. Bidwell.*

10. Frank Ninkovich, *The United States and Imperialism* (Malden, Mass.: Blackwell, 2001), 56; "Senator Jones Says the Main Question Will Be the Government of the Philippines," *New York Times*, June 18, 1901.

11. Deborah D. Herrera, "Unincorporated and Exploited: Differential Treatment for Trust Territory Claimants—Why Doesn't the Constitution Follow the Flag?" *Seton Hall Constitutional Law Journal* 2 (Spring 1992): 590–619; Christina Duffy Burnett and Burke Marshall, eds., *Foreign in a Domestic Sense: Puerto Rico, American Expansion, and the Constitution* (Durham, N.C.: Duke University Press, 2001).

12. Judge Thomas K. Moore, U.S. Virgin Islands, in a memorandum on *Krim M. Ballentine v. United States of America*, District Court of the U.S. Virgin Islands, Division of St. Thomas and St. John, Civ. No. 1999-130 (2001), 21.

13. T. Alexander Aleinikoff, "Sovereignty Studies in Constitutional Law," *Constitutional Commentary* 17 (Summer 2000): 197–204; Gerald L. Neuman, *Strangers to the Constitution: Immigrants, Borders and Fundamental Law* (Princeton, N.J.: Princeton University Press, 1996), 189.

14. *Shafiq Rasul et al. v. George W. Bush, President of the United States, et al.*, 542 U.S. 466 (2004), opinion of the Court (Justice Stevens); concurring opinion (Justice Kennedy); dissenting opinion (Justice Scalia). The *Rasul* ruling anticipated *Lakhdar Boumediene et al. v. George W. Bush et al.*, 553 U.S. ___ (2008), which explicitly extends to the prisoners of Guantánamo Bay (over which, it states, Cuba "retains *de jure* sovereignty," but the United States "maintains *de facto* sovereignty") the constitutional right to go to federal court to challenge their detention.

15. Sanford Levinson, of the University of Texas Law School, quoted in Chris Mooney, "Second-Class Citizens: The Separate and Unequal Treatment of Our Far-Flung Territories," *Legal Affairs* (July–August 2003), http://www.legalaffairs.org/issues/July-August-2003/story_mooney_julaug03.msp (accessed January 10, 2008); Kal Raustiala, "Does the Constitution Follow the Flag? Iraq, the War on Terror, and the Reach of the Law," *UCLA Law* 26 (Winter 2004): 6–9.

NOTES TO CHAPTER 10

1. Karal Ann Marling and John Wetenhall, *Iwo Jima: Monuments, Memories and the American Hero* (Cambridge, Mass.: Harvard University Press, 1991).

2. Samuel Abbott, *The Dramatic Story of Old Glory* (New York: Boni and Liveright, 1919), 274, 279.

3. Daniela Rossini, *Il mito americano nell'Italia della Grande Guerra* (Rome-Bari: Laterza, 2000), 148–49, 132, 207–8.

4. William A. Williams, *America Confronts a Revolutionary World: 1776–1976* (New York: Morrow, 1976), 126.

5. Woodrow Wilson, "A League for Peace" or "Peace without Victory," address of President Wilson to the U.S. Senate, January 22, 1917, available online at http://www.sagehistory.net/worldwar1/docs/WWPeaceVict.htm (accessed February 19, 2008).

6. Marshall's words are inscribed in the northern wall of the World War Two Memorial, inaugurated in 2004 in the heart of the National Mall in Washington, D.C.

7. Red Army photographer Yevgeny Ananievich Khaldei, who shot the photograph on the roof of the Reichstag with a makeshift flag (actually a red tablecloth with a white cardboard hammer and sickle sewed on it), had admired Rosenthal's Iwo Jima picture in a magazine and wanted to do something as triumphal for the flag of his own country. See Mark Grosset, *Khaldei: Un photoreporter en Union Soviétique* (Paris: Editions du Chêne, 2004).

8. Henry Luce, "The American Century," *Life*, February 17, 1941, reprinted in *The Ideas of Henry Luce*, ed. John K. Jessup (New York: Atheneum, 1969), 105–20.

9. Karal Ann Mailing, *Norman Rockwell* (New York: Harry N. Abrams, 1997), 106; Laura Claridge, *Norman Rockwell: A Life* (New York: Random House, 2001), 321–22; Maureen Honey, *Creating Rosie the Riveter: Class, Gender, and Propaganda during World War II* (Amherst: University of Massachusetts Press, 1984).

10. Tom Wells, *The War Within: America's Battle over Vietnam* (Berkeley: University of California Press, 1994), 160, 179, 196, 277, 427, 542; Todd Gitlin, *The Sixties: Years of Hope, Years of Rage* (New York: Bantam Books, 1993), 394.

11. Henry David Thoreau, *Civil Disobedience, or Resistance to Civil Government* (1849), in *The Portable Thoreau*, ed. Carl Bode (New York: Penguin, 1975), 112–13, 120.

12. "Flag Burning Time!" website of Marc Perkel, http://www.perkel.com/politics/gore/recount.htm (accessed January 10, 2008).

13. Bodnar, *Remaking America*, 3–9; Kristin Ann Hass, *Carried to the Wall: American Memory and the Vietnam Veterans Memorial* (Berkeley: University of California Press, 1998).

14. "Vietnam Veterans Memorial," National Park Service website, http://www.nps.gov/vive/index.htm (accessed March 20, 2003). Years later, at the same website

(accessed February 14, 2008) one finds a new introduction: "Deliberately setting aside the controversies of the war, the Vietnam Veterans Memorial honors the men and women who served when their Nation called upon them. The designer, Maya Lin, felt that 'the politics had eclipsed the veterans, their service and their lives.' She kept the design elegantly simple to 'allow everyone to respond and remember.'"

NOTES TO CHAPTER 11

1. Robert H. Ferrell, "Presidential Leadership and International Aspects of the Space Program," in *Spaceflight and the Myth of Presidential Leadership*, ed. Roger D. Launius and Howard E. McCurdy (Urbana: University of Illinois Press, 1997), 178; President John F. Kennedy, "Address at Rice University on the Nation's Space Effort," September 12, 1962, Houston, Texas, available online at http://www.jfklibrary.org/Historical+Resources/Archives/Reference+Desk/Speeches/JFK/003POF03SpaceEffort09121962.htm (accessed February 19, 2008).

2. Max Frankel, "Soviet Rocket Hits Moon . . . Sphere Carries Pennants and Hammer and Sickle to Lunar Surface," *New York Times*, September 14, 1959; Peter Kihss, "U.S. Rejects Any Flag-Planting as Legal Claim to Rule Moon," *New York Times*, September 14, 1959; "Bringing Memento of Moon Shot: Gift to President," *New York Times*, September 15, 1959.

3. Quoted in Erik Barnouw, *Tube of Plenty: The Evolution of American Television* (New York: Oxford University Press, 1990), 249.

4. Buzz Aldrin on *The NewsHour with Jim Lehrer*, PBS-TV, July 20, 1999, transcript available online at http://www.pbs.org/newshour/bb/science/july-dec99/apollo_7-20a.html (accessed February 19, 2008).

5. Article 2, "Treaty on Principles Governing the Activities of States in the Exploration and Use of Outer Space, Including the Moon and Other Celestial Bodies" (1967), in *United Nations Treaties and Principles on Outer Space* (New York: United Nations, 2005), 5.

6. President Ronald Reagan, "Remarks at a Flag Day Ceremony," June 14, 1985, Baltimore, Maryland, available online at http://www.reagan.utexas.edu/archives/speeches/1985/61485f.htm (accessed February 14, 2008).

7. Jon Nordheimer, "Flag on July 4: Thrill to Some, Threat to Others," *New York Times*, July 4, 1969.

8. Nell Irving Painter, *Creating Black Americans: African American History and Its Meanings, 1619 to the Present* (New York: Oxford University Press, 2006), 308–9.

9. Roger Launius on *The NewsHour with Jim Lehrer*, PBS-TV, February 4, 2003, transcript available online at http://www.pbs.org/newshour/bb/science/jan-june03/

columbia_2-4.html (accessed February 19, 2008); Leepson, *Flag: An American Biography*, 239. And yet the NASA studies of the early 1960s on human missions to Mars and Venus were known as Project EMPIRE (Early Manned Planetary-Interplanetary Roundtrip Expedition). See Anne M. Platoff, "Eyes on the Red Planet: Human Mars Mission Planning, 1952–1970," report prepared for the Lyndon B. Johnson Space Center, July 2001, available online at ston.jsc.nasa.gov/collections/TRS/_techrep/CR-2001-208928.pdf (accessed July 4, 2009).

10. "Armstrong Will Place U.S. Flag on the Moon," *New York Times*, June 22, 1969; "What Flag(s) on the Moon?" (editorial), *New York Times*, June 23, 1969.

11. Quoted in Ferrell, "Presidential Leadership," 178–79.

12. Anne M. Platoff, "Where No Flag Has Gone Before: Political and Technical Aspects of Placing a Flag on the Moon," paper prepared for the Lyndon B. Johnson Space Center, August 1993, available online at http://www.jsc.nasa.gov/history/flag/flag.htm (accessed February 19, 2008).

13. Edwin E. Aldrin, Jr., "Lunar Dust Smelled Just Like Gunpowder," *Life*, August 22, 1969, 26.

NOTES TO CHAPTER 12

1. Robert J. Goldstein, *Saving "Old Glory": The History of the American Flag Desecration Controversy* (Boulder, Colo.: Westview, 1995); Robert J. Goldstein, *Burning the Flag: The Great 1989–1990 Flag Desecration Controversy* (Kent, Ohio: Kent State University Press, 1996); Robert J. Goldstein, *Flag Burning and Free Speech: The Case of Texas v. Johnson* (Lawrence: University Press of Kansas, 2000); *The Constitution and the Flag*, vol. 2, *The Flag Burning Cases*, ed. Michael K. Curtis (New York: Garland, 1993).

2. The text of the 1968 Federal Flag Desecration Law (18 U.S.C. §700(b) [1988]) is in Goldstein, *Burning the Flag*, 413.

3. *Spence v. Washington*, 418 U.S. 405 (1974).

4. *Texas v. Johnson*, 491 U.S. 397 (1989); concurring opinion (Justice Kennedy).

5. *United States v. Eichman*, 496 U.S. 310 (1990).

6. Quoted in Goldstein, *Burning the Flag*, 72.

7. Hendrik Hertzberg, "For Which It Stands," *New Yorker*, July 3, 2006, 49.

8. Carl Hulse, "Flag Amendment Narrowly Fails in Senate Vote," *New York Times*, June 28, 2006.

9. "Obama Statement on Flag Burning Amendment," press release, June 27, 2006, available online at http://obama.senate.gov/press/060627-obama_statement_29/ (accessed February 23, 2008). The then-senator from New York, Hillary

Rodham Clinton, voted against the amendment but cosponsored legislation that would have criminalized flag desecration. See Anne E. Kornblut, "Senator Clinton and Liberals Split over Flag Desecration," *New York Times*, June 28, 2006.

10. Sheryl Gay Stolberg, "Given New Legs, an Old Idea Is Back," *New York Times*, June 4, 2003; John M. Broder, "Lawmaker Quits after He Pleads Guilty to Bribes," *New York Times*, November 29, 2005; Randal C. Archibold, "Ex-Congressman Gets 8-Year Term in Bribery Case," *New York Times*, March 4, 2006.

NOTES TO CHAPTER 13

1. Ilene Susan Fort, *The Flag Paintings of Childe Hassan* (Los Angeles: Los Angeles County Museum of Art, 1988).

2. Quoted in Guenter, *The American Flag*, 157.

3. Albert Boime, *The Unveiling of the National Icons: A Plea for Patriotic Iconoclasm in a Nationalist Era* (New York: Cambridge University Press, 1998), 43–81; *Old Glory: The American Flag in Contemporary Art*, ed. David S. Rubin (Cleveland, Ohio: Cleveland Center for Contemporary Art, 1994).

4. Roberta Bernstein, *Jasper Johns' Paintings and Sculptures, 1954–1974* (Ann Arbor, Mich.: UMI Research Press, 1985), 1–15.

5. Todd Gitlin, *The Whole World Is Watching: Mass Media in the Making and Unmaking of the New Left* (Berkeley: University of California Press, 1980), 171–74; Stephen J. Whitfield, "The Stunt Man: Abbie Hoffman (1936–1989)," in *Sights on the Sixties*, ed. Barbara L. Tischler (New Brunswick, N.J.: Rutgers University Press, 1992), 103–19.

6. *Hair: The American Tribe Love-Rock Musical*, lyrics by Gerome Ragni and James Rado, music by Galt McDermot (New York: Pocket Books, 1970), 98.

7. Johnny Black, *Jimi Hendrix: The Ultimate Experience* (New York: Thunder's Mouth, 1999), 201.

8. Quoted in Michael Kiefer, "Tempest in a Toilet Bowl," *Phoenix New Times*, June 6, 1996.

9. *Faith Ringgold: Twenty Years of Painting, Sculpture and Performance, 1963–1983* (New York: Studio Museum of Harlem, 1984); *David Hammons: Rousing the Rubble* (New York: Institute of Contemporary Art, P.S. 1 Museum, 1991).

10. Quoted in Elsa Honig Fine, *The Afro-American Artist* (New York: Holt, Rinehart & Winston, 1973) 209, 206.

11. Steven C. Dubin, *Arresting Images: Impolitic Art and Uncivil Actions* (New York: Routledge, 1992), 102–24.

12. Michael Kiefer, "Legionnaire's Disease," *Phoenix New Times*, April 4, 1996;

Kathleen Vanesian, "Deja Wow: Red, White and Snooze," *Phoenix New Times*, April 4, 1996; B. Drummond Ayres, Jr., "Art or Trash? Arizona Exhibit on American Flag Unleashes a Controversy," *New York Times*, June 8, 1996.

13. Lawrence H. Suid and Dolores A. Haverstick, *Stars and Stripes on Screen: A Comprehensive Guide to Portrayals of American Military on Film* (Lanham, Md.: Scarecrow, 2005) is a compendium of fourteen hundred Hollywood war motion pictures, replete with flags and flag-raising glories; but war movies, of course, do not have a monopoly on the representation of the flag.

14. Ann Patchett, "The Country of Country," *New York Times Magazine*, May 11, 2003, 15–16.

NOTES TO CHAPTER 14

1. Alessandra Mauro, "11 settembre un anno dopo: Quali immagini restano," *Acoma: Rivista Internazionale di Studi Nordamericani* 25 (Winter 2003): 112–22.

2. Kevin Flynn, "Ground Zero, a Memorial: Firefighters Block a Plan for Statue in Brooklyn," *New York Times*, January 18, 2002.

3. Carroll Doherty, "Who Flies the Flag? Not Always Who You Might Think," Pew Research Center for the People and the Press, June 27, 2007, available online at http://pewresearch.org/pubs/525/who-flies-the-flag-not-always-who-you-might-think (accessed February 14, 2008).

4. Susan Willis, "Old Glory" (2002), in *Portents of the Real: A Primer for Post-9/11 America* (New York: Verso, 2005), 13.

5. Rick Hampson, "Mystery Drapes Flag's Disappearance," *USA Today*, August 31, 2006; Help Find the Flag website, http://www.findthe911flag.com/ (accessed February 18, 2008).

6. Jim Dwyer, "Troops Told to Carry Freedom, Not the Flag," *New York Times*, March 20, 2003; Brian Whitaker, "Flags in the Dust," *Guardian*, March 24, 2003.

7. Andy Newman, "Atop Statue, Marine Thrills Army of Fans Back Home," *New York Times*, April 11, 2003; Bernard Weinraub, "Display of U.S. Flag Barred after Unfurling on Statue," *New York Times*, April 11, 2003.

8. A 2004 Dick Wright syndicated cartoon depicts Uncle Sam looking at an American flag soiled with a "U.S. abuse of Iraqi prisoners" stain and thinking, "It'll take more than a strong detergent to get this stain out." *Gwinnett Daily Post*, May 5, 2004.

9. Niall Ferguson, "The Empire Slinks Back," *New York Times Magazine*, April 27, 2003, 7; Norman Mailer, "Only in America," *New York Review of Books*, March 27, 2003, 49–53.

10. Randolph S. Bourne, "The War and the Intellectuals" (1917), in *War and the Intellectuals*, 10.

11. Francesco Dragosei, *Lo squalo e il grattacielo: Miti e fantasmi dell'immaginario americano* (Bologna: Il Mulino, 2002).

12. Dinesh D'Souza, "Why They Hate Us: America and Its Enemies," in *What's So Great about America* (New York: Penguin, 2003), 3–35; Daniel J. Flynn, *Why the Left Hates America* (New York: Random House, 2002); Dinesh D'Souza, "Why Liberals Hate America," in *Letters to a Young Conservative* (New York: Basic Books, 2002), 205–9.

13. Peggy Noonan, *A Heart, a Cross, and a Flag: America Today* (New York: Free Press, 2003).

14. Toby Keith, "Courtesy of the Red, White, and Blue," *Unleashed*, 2002; Darryl Worley, "Have You Forgotten?" *Have You Forgotten?* 2003; Lynyrd Skynyrd, "Red, White, and Blue," *Vicious Cycle*, 2003.

15. Willis, "Old Glory," 20.

16. Quoted in Stuart Elliott, "Another Wave of Patriotic Marketing," *New York Times*, March 26, 2003; see also Ames Boykin, "American Flag Sales Hold Steady but They're Not Flying Off the Shelves Like after Sept. 11," *Chicago Daily Herald*, April 2, 2003.

17. Todd Gitlin, *The Intellectuals and the Flag* (New York: Columbia University Press, 2005), 155; Katha Pollitt, "Put Out No Flags," *Nation*, October 8, 2001, 7; Erica Jong, "Wrapped in the Flag" (2002), available online at http://www.ericajong.com/wrappedintheflag.htm (accessed February 14, 2008).

18. Barbara Kingsolver, "And Our Flag Was Still There," in *Small Wonder: Essays* (New York: HarperCollins, 2002), 236, 238.

19. Arthur M. Schlesinger, Jr., "Who Owns Old Glory?" *Rolling Stone*, May 15, 2003, 71; Bill Moyers, "Reclaiming the Flag," *Rolling Stone*, May 15, 2003, 72.

20. Gore Vidal, "We Are the Patriots," *Nation*, June 2, 2003, 1.

21. Michael Kazin, "A Patriotic Left," *Dissent* 49 (Fall 2002): 41–44; Michael Wreszin, "Confessions of an 'Anti-American,'" *Dissent* 50 (Spring 2003): 83–86; Gitlin, *Intellectuals and the Flag*.

22. Dean E. Murphy, "Patriot Games: Look Who's Embracing Flag and Country," *New York Times*, March 30, 2003; Robert Salladay, "Anti-war Patriots Find They Need to Reclaim Words, Symbols, Even U.S. Flag from Conservatives," *San Francisco Chronicle*, April 7, 2003.

Index

About the Author

Arnaldo Testi is Professor of U.S. History at the University of Pisa and has written numerous books on American history.